Walking the Disused Railways of Kent

David Bathurst

Photographs by David Bathurst

S.B. Publications

By the same author:

The Selsey Tram
Six Of The Best
The Jennings Companion
Financial Penalties
Around Chichester In Old Photographs
Here's A Pretty Mess!
Magisterial Lore
The Beaten Track (republished as The Big Walks Of Great Britain)
Poetic Justice
That's My Girl
Walking The Coastline Of Sussex
Best Sussex Walks
Let's Take It From The Top
Walking The Disused Railways Of Sussex
Once More From The Top
Sussex Top Tens
Walking The Kent Coast From End To End
Walking The South Coast Of England
Walking The Riversides Of Sussex
Anyone For Tenors?
Walking The Triangulation Points Of Sussex

To Chris and Alison

First published in 2010 by S.B. Publications
14 Bishopstone Road, Seaford, East Sussex.
Tel: 01323 893498   Email: sbpublications@tiscali.co.uk

ISBN 978-1-85770-356-6

Typeset by EH Graphics, East Sussex (01273) 515527

CONTENTS

Front Cover: The Tenterden to Headcorn line on the approach to Biddenden.

Title Page: An overbridge on the Paddock Wood-Hawkhurst line just beyond Cranbrook station.

Back Cover: Looking towards Chatham across land along which the Rochester Bridge-Chatham Central line ran - ending nowhere near the centre of Chatham!

ACKNOWLEDGMENTS

I would like to thank Lindsay Woods of SB Publications for her encouragement and support; the owners of The Chase at Bay View on Sheppey who allowed me access to a section of disused railway through their property; and my wife Susan and daughter Jennifer who have coped admirably with my very early starts from our Sussex home to explore some of the more far-flung parts of Kent!

ABOUT THE AUTHOR

David Bathurst was born in 1959 and has enjoyed writing and walking throughout his adult life. He has walked all the complete official long-distance footpaths of Great Britain including the South West Coast Path, the Pennine Way and Offa's Dyke Path, and he has also walked the entire south coast of England, his guides to the Sussex and Kent coasts being published by SB Publications in 2002 and 2007 respectively. By profession David is a solicitor and legal adviser to magistrates in Chichester and Worthing. He is married to Susan and has a daughter Jennifer. When not writing or walking he loves vintage sitcom, teashops, and the Times crossword puzzle. His most notable achievements have been the recital of the four Gospels from memory on a single day in 1998 and the recital of the complete works of Gilbert & Sullivan from memory over 4 days in 2007.

INTRODUCTION

Although Great Britain is still well served by rail, there are a considerable number of lines that have fallen into disuse. The pattern is distressingly familiar: conception, construction and opening during the colossal railway-building boom in the latter half of the 19th century, prosperity for a while, and then steady decline in the face of ever-increasing competition from the roads. The fact that the lines closed so long ago means there is often little, if any, trace of them; however, a good deal of evidence of the lines, in the form of bridges, tunnels, embankments, cuttings and even station buildings, still remains, and often it is possible to trace sections of the old lines themselves on the ground. Exploring these old lines, and their fate since closure, on foot, is a fascinating way of keeping in touch with a very important part of our heritage while providing interesting and fulfilling walking in often most attractive scenery. It has deservedly become very popular in the last 20 or 30 years, its popularity boosted by the recent BBC television series (now available on DVD) on walking disused railways.

The aim of this book is to provide a definitive guide to walking the many disused railway lines of Kent. My original intention was to describe walking routes along every piece of disused railway in Kent. However, even a cursory glance at railway maps of Kent would demonstrate the impossibility of this task. It would have meant including not only numerous defunct industrial, dockyard and military lines, but also old alignments, disused platforms, disused sections of track, sidings and spur routes of existing lines, many of them inaccessible to walkers and providing walking that was either non-existent or wholly unrewarding. But to have restricted myself to lines that formed part of the passenger network would have meant excluding some very fine railway walking indeed. I have therefore compromised. I have indeed included all the disused railway lines that formed part of the passenger network, excluding only old alignments, spurs and sidings which could not be said to create new branches with discrete identities or characters of their own. (The only exception is the now disused spur linking the Folkestone-Dover line with Folkestone Harbour which is of particular interest as a newly-disused piece of railway and which forms a convenient "tailpiece" to the chapter devoted to the Elham Valley Line.) In addition, however, I have included all the "non-passenger" lines that feature in the Gazetteer of disused railways in the South East edition of what is arguably the definitive guide to the subject, H.P. White's Forgotten Railways series. (It is of note that authorisation was obtained to convey passengers on some of these "freight only" lines, meaning they could easily have become incorporated into the passenger network.) Each of the walks described provide some very fine and rewarding exploration, and completion of all of them will give you a very full picture of the disused railway scene in Kent as well as provide walking through some of the county's prettiest towns, villages and countryside.

The book is divided into seventeen chapters. Most chapters are devoted to a single line each, but on occasion it is convenient to cover more than one line in a chapter. Each chapter starts with essential information for walkers, then there's a brief history of the line or lines being described in the chapter, leading on to the full description of the walking route or routes to which the chapter relates. The start and finish points of each walk are at places that are well served by public transport, usually (but by no means always) rail transport. Times have changed. H.P. White, writing in 1976, remarked that the "very best way" to visit the courses of the old lines was by car. These days, to suggest such a thing borders on the irresponsible; in any case, it may prove very inconvenient to undertake one of the linear walks described in the book and then have to find your way back to your car at the end. Using public transport is not only far more environmentally responsible but provides flexibility and makes for a more relaxing day out - providing, of course, that you do your homework, check times carefully and allow more time than you need in case of unforeseen delay. Four of the walks actually begin at or go through places to or from which a steam train journey can be undertaken, providing a perfect complement to the walk (these being New Romney, Tenterden, Eythorne and Tunbridge Wells West).

The aim is to provide a series of walks that follow, as far as is possible, the actual courses of the old lines. However, one thing that needs to be made clear from the start is that much - indeed, the majority - of the walking will not be on the courses of the old lines themselves. Unfortunately, only a very small amount of former trackbed in Kent is now available to the public as rights of way. Whereas in many other counties large sections of old railway tracks have been turned into public footpaths and cycleways by enlightened local councils, that is very much the exception in Kent. If you were to confine yourself to walking only along officially designated public rights of way, you would end up doing only a negligible amount of walking on the old lines themselves. Inevitably there does need to be recourse to some sections which are not officially marked on maps as rights of way and where accessing and following them may not always be completely discomfort-free. Seasoned disused railway walkers would say that was all part of the fun! That said, the routes described in this book have been carefully prepared and researched to ensure that "legitimate" alternatives are used wherever possible and practicable, including occasions when following the old line with the eyes may in fact prove more rewarding than trying to struggle along it. It is pointless, for instance, to send you across a heavily cultivated field just to say you have been on the old line when there's a quiet road running immediately adjacent to and within sight of it. In all cases, however, sections of old line that are not designated rights of way are avoided where accessing or following them is physically impossible, may (by virtue of obstructions or terrain to be crossed) pose a significant danger or unreasonable discomfort to the walker (you should never be expected to surmount a barbed wire fence, for instance), may cause a significant risk of damage to property (including your own), may constitute a criminal offence(e.g. trespassing onto railway or Ministry of Defence property) or may constitute a fundamental breach of landowners' privacy.

That still leaves a number of sections described in this book which may give rise to concern. The safest course is always to seek permission from the owner before walking over a piece of land that is not designated as a right of way. That is a counsel of perfection; in many cases common-sense will tell you that there will be no difficulty, but if in the slightest doubt it is better to make enquiries and secure permission rather than risk the embarrassment of being challenged by irate landowners, especially if you are contravening a "Keep Out" sign! Do not think you will always get away with taking the risk, as I know from personal experience (I will say no more than that) that you will not. The relevant sections in the book, by the use of the words "please refer to my introductory notes"(or similar), will make it clear when you are being directed across land which you would do well to consider seeking permission to enter. On occasion, I have specifically indicated that permission MUST be sought to walk a particular section. For the avoidance of doubt, neither my publishers nor myself can accept any responsibility for the consequences of your trespassing onto land that is not designated as a right of way, without having obtained permission in advance. Moreover, whilst every effort has been made to ensure the information provided is accurate, land use does change frequently and there may be sections of old line which were inaccessible at the time of writing but which you find to be available, while conversely you may find certain previously accessible sections obstructed when you come to walk them. I therefore recommend you equip yourself with a map before setting out, so that if the way as described in my text is impassable, you can plan and execute an alternative route. Sketch maps are provided at the start of each chapter but an Ordnance Survey map of the section you are covering (the Explorer maps are the best), as well as assisting you if you find yourself with unexpected access problems, will add to the enjoyment of your walk as you can identify places of scenic and historic interest in the surrounding area.

The walks vary in length and difficulty. I suggest you read the introductory sections carefully before opting for a particular walk described in the text that follows. Mileage is only one factor to consider; you also need to take conditions and public transport/refreshment availability into account. There are some walks such as Strood-Chatham Central that are ideal for a family walk or an afternoon stroll; some that are pleasant short half-day excursions such as Sandling-Sandgate; while others, including the New Romney-Dungeness walk, are logistically demanding, involve some tricky route-finding and could prove very tiring for walkers who are insufficiently prepared. By definition most of the walking is on the flat, but there are some undulating sections and one or two quite stiff climbs and steep descents. In some places the surrounding vegetation and undergrowth can be quite dense, and although the walks described do not take you through impenetrable terrain, you would be well advised to attire yourself in reasonably stout clothing and footwear. Heavy walking boots are not necessary or recommended; comfortable walking shoes or light boots are best. All the normal advice to those undertaking a walk in the countryside applies. Take plenty of refreshment with you, particularly drinking water, and also food on longer walks where the section introductions indicate a paucity of pubs, shops and cafes. And bearing in mind that you'll need to get home again afterwards, always check public transport availability and times very carefully, and have the numbers of local taxi firms handy just in case. Providing you take these simple precautions you should enjoy some lovely and thoroughly rewarding exploration of railways that once graced the so-called Garden of England.

Happy walking.

PUBLIC TRANSPORT
Buses
Just three bus operators provide services referred to in the text, although please note that services are either greatly reduced or non-existent on Sundays and Bank Holidays. The relevant operator is indicated by initials in the preamble to each walk.

SC - Stagecoach 0845 121 0170 www.stagecoachbus.com
ARR - Arriva 0871 200 2233 www.arrivabus.co.uk
ESCC - East Sussex County Council Rider 0871 200 2233 www.eastsussex.gov.uk

Timetables for most routes are posted on the websites shown above.
My own experience is that the buses are extremely reliable, but it may still be prudent to have the number of local taxi firms handy, just in case!

Trains
Except where stated in the text, all the train services referred to in the text are provided by South-Eastern Trains. All provide a Sunday and Bank Holiday service but often there is weekend engineering work with trains being replaced by buses. For more information ring National Rail Enquiries on 08457 484950.

REFRESHMENTS
The availability of refreshments is shown in the pre-amble to each walk with the following abbreviations used.
P - pub or pubs
S - foodstore or stores
C - café or cafes
Please note that the information provided was correct at the time of writing but changes cannot be ruled out.

LOCATION OF WALKS

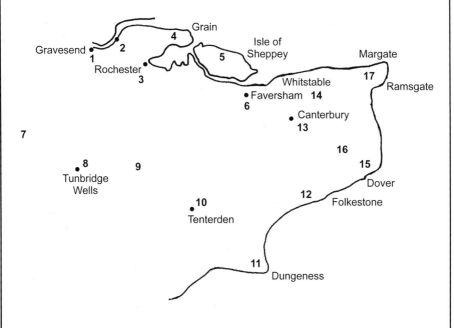

1	Gravesend - Fawkham Junction
2	Chattenden and Kingsnorth Railways
3	Rochester Bridge - Chatham Central
4	Stoke - Allhallows
5	Isle of Sheppey
6	Faversham Quay
7	Westerham - Dunton Green
8	Tunbridge Wells West - Grove Junction
9	Paddock Wood - Hawkhurst
10	Tenterden - Headcorn
11	New Romney and Dungeness
12	Sandling - Sandgate
13	Elham Valley Line and Folkestone Harbour
14	Canterbury - Whitstable
15	Martin Mill - Dover
16	East Kent Colliery Lines
17	Ramsgate - Margate

WALK 1 - **GRAVESEND - FAWKHAM JUNCTION**

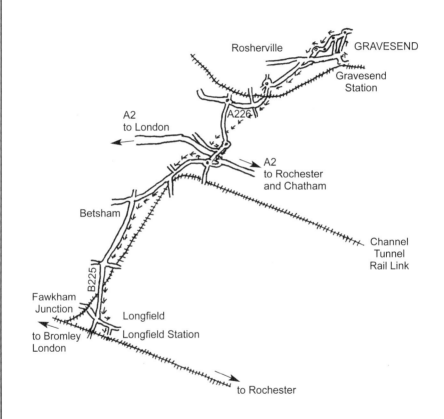

Rosherville   GRAVESEND

Gravesend
Station

A2
to London

A226

A2
to Rochester
and Chatham

Betsham

Channel
Tunnel
Rail Link

Fawkham
Junction

B225

Longfield

to Bromley
London

Longfield Station

to Rochester

Scale: 2cm - 1km

WALK 1 - GRAVESEND - FAWKHAM JUNCTION

Length:	6 miles.
Start:	Gravesend station.
Finish:	Longfield station.
Public Transport:	Regular trains serving Gravesend on London Charing Cross-Gillingham line; regular trains serving Longfield on Rochester-London Victoria line.
Refreshments:	Gravesend (P,C,S); Pepper Hill (C); Longfield (P,C,S).
Conditions:	This is a walk of three parts. The first is disappointing road-walking, with very little of interest to see once you've left the riverside. The second provides some excellent old railway walking and it is worth undertaking the whole of this walk just for that. The third is back on roads, but is interesting as you will see a rare example of a railway of the past becoming a railway of the future. The whole walk is comfortably manageable by most walkers within half a day.

History

Gravesend had enjoyed a rail link since 1849 in the form of the North Kent line, which we know today as that linking Gillingham, Rochester and Strood with London Charing Cross. In 1881, however, the Gravesend Railway Company was formed to build a branch to Gravesend from Fawkham Junction, just west of Longfield on the London Victoria-Rochester-Dover line owned by the London Chatham & Dover Railway (LCDR). The LCDR in fact took over the Gravesend Railway Company and the branch duly opened in spring 1886, the first trains running on 10 May. The northern terminus was at a station that came to be known as Gravesend West Street, later still Gravesend West, as the line - travelling roughly south to north - was entirely separate from the North Kent line (which went west to east), and there was an adjoining pier (with separate platform) from which ferries travelled daily to Rotterdam. Intermediate stations, from Fawkham Junction on the main London Victoria-Dover line, were provided at Longfield Halt, Southfleet and Rosherville, adjoining the then famous Rosherville pleasure gardens which ironically closed in 1890. It is hardly surprising that Rosherville station, which was just half a mile short of the terminus, shut in 1933. Services were initially frequent but by 1909 only half a dozen down trains, all coming from London, were serving the line. After the line was electrified in 1939 through services from London ceased, with Gravesend-bound trains starting from Farningham Road or Swanley, and the line finally closed to passengers on 3 August 1953. However freight services - there was a connection to a nearby paper mill and also coal sidings - continued until 1968 when the section between Southfleet and Gravesend West shut altogether. Freight services then continued from Fawkham Junction to Southfleet, where a coal railhead was set up, but now this section of the old line is being redeveloped as part of a plan to provide fast rail links from the Continent and from Kent itself into London.

Walking the Line

This walk is described from Gravesend southwards. Make your way out of Gravesend station via the north exit into Clive Road, turning left and immediately right into Bath Street; follow it downhill away from the main shopping area, then turn second left into Clifton Street, following it to Stuart Road at its junction with West Street. Looking ahead towards the river, you'll see what is left of the old pier, the bridge which until quite recently linked the pier with the land below the superstores and industrial units to the left having been severed. Gravesend West station would have been sited just to your left at this point, immediately to the west of Stuart Road at its bottom end. Go past the pier and immediately beyond it bear left into Thames Way, keeping to your left the embankment on which the old line was built. It's possible to scramble up onto the embankment but there's no path to speak of. Return to Thames Way and follow it, passing under a bridge and going uphill to arrive at a T-junction with the A226. The

The sad remains of the pier just beyond Gravesend West, the start and finish of the Gravesend-Fawkham Junction line, on the banks of the Thames.

old Rosherville station was sited hereabouts, but all traces of the old line have been completely obliterated among the new roads. At the T-junction, turn left to follow the busy A226, which fortunately has a pavement; there is no trace at all of the old line, albeit the A226 follows its course at this point. The A226 bends slightly right, veering away from the course of the old line, and arrives at a roundabout. Bear left (first exit) to pass under a road bridge and then the bridge of the extant London-Gravesend line, heading south-westwards, the course of the old line going parallel with you to the left but completely impossible to discern. However, things now look up. Just a couple of hundred yards beyond the railway overbridge you reach a junction with Vale Road; go over this junction and a little beyond it, veer left onto a cycle track, the police station just ahead of you. As you follow the cycle track, the old railway

Tangles of vegetation flank a clearly-defined section of the old line between Gravesend and Southfleet.

embankment is immediately beside you to your left, and it is possible to mount the embankment and gain access to the old line. More energetic walkers will be happy to scramble up the embankment at the first opportunity, but it is possible to obtain gentler passage to the embankment by following the cycle path on to a proper crossing point. You can first follow the old line back towards the Vale Road crossing, but you're beaten back by the vegetation, so now turn back and walk south-westwards along the course of the old line; it's very clearly defined with no obstructions, and although it doesn't appear on maps as a right of way, it is not only accessible but very pleasant walking indeed.

Continue along the obvious course of the line in the shade of trees, briefly leaving the course of the old line in order to climb up to Springhead Road, about half a mile from Vale Road. Cross over Springhead Road and turn left, then bear immediately right down a narrow path - at the time of writing a large stone slab marked the path entrance. The

The highlight of the walk between Gravesend and Fawkham Junction - this magnificent overbridge just north of the A2 crossing.

path drops down through quite thick vegetation and soon you're back on the course of the old line, heading south-westwards; this really is delightful walking in the shade of trees, with banks rising up steeply on both sides, and there's the bonus of a splendid overbridge above you. However, less than half a mile from Springhead Road, you emerge from the trees to find yourself at the top of a grassy bank with the A2 below you, and in fact you can easily discern the course of the old line on the other side of the road! Do not even think about crossing the A2, though, but instead make your way down to the roadside and turn left to follow a safe footpath which follows a slip road leading away from the A2 to a junction with the A260 Hall Road at Pepper Hill. Turn right to cross a bridge over the A2, with pavements thankfully provided, and then take the first right turn, the B262 Station Road for Betsham and Green Street Green. Just to your right here is a garden centre, within which there is an excellent café offering the only on-route refreshment opportunity - really too good to miss! Immediately beyond the garden centre is a fruit farm. If the fruit farm is open, turn right to follow the main access track, which helpfully goes up to and follows the left side of the course of the old line (note a fine bridge carrying the line over a gap in the embankment) and, better still, entry onto the course of the old line is possible from the track not far short of the car park. Although the course is not always clearly defined, it is possible for you to bear right to follow the old line back towards the A2. Do be careful though, as at one point the "path" along the embankment seems to give out among impenetrable vegetation and you need to alter your course slightly which will involve negotiating miscellaneous pieces of loose debris, some natural, some very definitely man-made. Then retrace your steps to where you joined the line, and continue along it, the path quite well defined throughout; it is not designated as a right of way, so please refer to my introductory notes. All too soon, barely a quarter of a mile from the joining point, the old line meets Station Road and you're forced off it, having to bear left just before the line meets the road and scramble through the vegetation to join the road*. Incidentally, Southfleet station was sited just here, on this (north) side of Station Road. If the fruit farm is shut, you will need to walk all the way along Station Road from the garden centre and access the old line from this (asterisked) point, backtracking to the A2 then returning to the asterisked point the same way.

Go briefly south-westwards along Station Road to the crossroads and turn left into Dale Road, and almost immediately you will cross over the course of the old line again, but now as a modern railway line complete with tracks and overhead electrical wires. This signifies that far from being part of railway history, the south-westward continuation of the old line is being reintegrated into the rail network and part of the extensive overhaul of the rail network in Kent designed to provide very speedy access to London for both Kent commuters and Channel Tunnel users. This continuation runs as far as Fawkham Junction, its junction with the well-established London-Rochester-Faversham line just west of Longfield. The fact that the track has been revitalised obviously makes it impossible for walkers to proceed along it, so backtrack to the crossroads and turn left along Station Road to Betsham half a mile away. At the village crossroads turn left along Westwood Road for roughly a mile to another crossroads; go straight over onto the B255 Whitehill Road, soon crossing over the "old" line again and descending to the village of Longfield. Turn left at the junction at the bottom of the hill along Main Road and then shortly right into Station Road, where not only will you find shops but a station at the top end, from which there are very good services on the London-Rochester-Faversham line.

WALK 2 - CHATTENDEN AND KINGSNORTH RAILWAYS

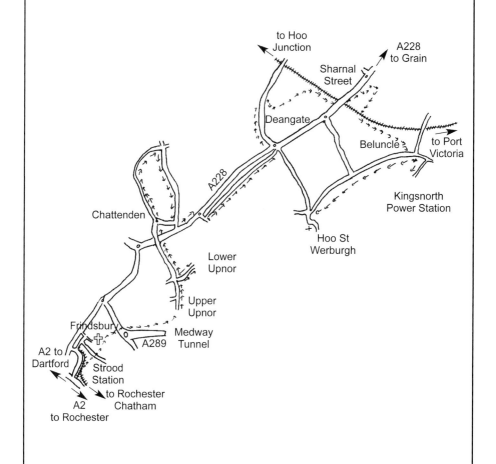

Scale: 3cm - 1km

WALK 2 - CHATTENDEN AND
KINGSNORTH RAILWAYS

Length:	Approximately 13 miles if this walk is undertaken in full; 7 miles if Chattenden Naval Tramway section alone is undertaken.
Start:	Strood station (complete walk); Hoo St Werburgh (Chattenden Naval Tramway section).
Finish:	Hoo St Werburgh (although note it is possible to link the walk with the Stoke-Allhallows walk: see description below)
Public Transport:	Regular trains serving Strood on London Charing Cross-Gillingham line; regular buses(ARR) serving Hoo St Werburgh on Strood-Grain route.
Refreshments:	Strood (P,C,S): Upnor(P); Ratcliffe Highway (P); Kingsnorth (C); Hoo St Werburgh (P,S).
Conditions:	The first part of the walk, following the Chattenden & Upnor Railway, involves almost exclusively road tramping, and is for the connoisseur only! The second part of the walk, following the Chattenden Naval Tramway, also involves some road walking but is far more interesting, especially as it involves a brief encounter with the quite delightful single-track Hoo-Port Victoria line. Thankfully it is possible to split the walk so you could just confine yourself to the Tramway if you wished. If you decide to do the lot, it will need at least a full day's walking, possibly more if public transport availability (or lack of) precludes an early start. The Tramway section in isolation can be accomplished within half a day.

History

The Chattenden & Upnor Railway, as it was called, was laid out for training purposes by the Royal Engineers shortly before the Boer War around the start of the 20th century. The line was taken over by the Admiralty in 1904. It was a 2ft 6in gauge which started by the Medway south of the village of Upper Upnor (there was a separate branch leading up from a pier at Lower Upnor) and went round Chattenden Barracks to arrive at the ammunition dump at Lodge Hill. Although it went into decline during the 1930's, it was resuscitated during World War 2, was dieselised after the war and survived until the last day of 1961. Another line, the Chattenden Naval Tramway, was opened in 1901, running from Lodge Hill to Sharnal Street where it connected with the Hoo Junction-Port Victoria line (see Stoke-Allhallows section), and then in 1915 it was extended to Kingsnorth Pier to serve aircraft hangers and a munitions factory. After World War 1 part of the munitions factory and the extended part of the line was leased to a chemical firm. Things were looking good for the Tramway, and in late 1926 authorisation was obtained to run passenger services along it, with ownership of the line beyond Sharnal Street being transferred to a Light Railway Company. Appropriately, the section of Tramway east of Sharnal Street became known as the Kingsnorth Light Railway. However no passenger service was ever set up, the chemical firm ceased to operate, and the Tramway closed after World War 2 - the Light Railway section from Sharnal Street to Kingsnorth sometime in the 12 years after the war, and the Tramway section from Lodge Hill to Sharnal Street in the early 1960's. All traces of it have now been obliterated with only one small section that is recognisable as part of an old railway line.

Walking the Line

If you want to do the whole thing, please read on. If you wish to confine yourself to the Naval Tramway section only, please start from the italicised section below. From Strood station, walk down the station approach road and bear left into Canal Road, going forward onto a footpath which emerges onto Wingrove Drive. Follow the drive to a junction with Commissioners Road which you cross straight over, going quite steeply up a footpath, then pass to the east of the hilltop Frindsbury church and arrive at a junction with Parsonage Lane. Turn right into the lane; you soon pass a footpath going off to the left, and immediately beyond this the road bends right. As it does so, look out for and then follow a signed footpath leading off to the right, going downhill to a roundabout junction.

Cross over the A289 using the crossing point to the left (north-west) of the roundabout, and from here, go straight ahead eastwards along a clear path running parallel with the A289 as it heads down towards the Medway Tunnel. The path swings north-eastwards away from the A289, keeping extensive works to the right, then goes forward to reach a road; it is the start of the road which roughly coincides with the start of the Upper Upnor branch of the Chattenden & Upnor Railway. You follow it northwards, passing the turning to the very attractive High Street which is to your right, leading down to the Medway estuary. Ignoring Upnor Road going off left, continue north-eastwards along the road away from Upnor - signs indicate that this is an MOD road and liable to be closed at certain times - and, remaining beside the course of the old line which ran just parallel with this road to the left, you go forward to a crossroads with a church to the left. By turning right at this crossroads and following the road down to the waterside, you are following beside the course of the branch of the Chattenden & Upnor line which started near the pier at Lower Upnor. It's worth walking to Lower Upnor, which you shortly reach, to enjoy its pretty quayside, even though there are no traces of the old line whatsoever. Return to the crossroads - going straight on if you didn't make the Lower Upnor detour, going right if you did - and continue along Upchat Road north-westwards to cross over the A228 by means of a bridge, swinging right to arrive at a roundabout junction* at the village of Chattenden.

Here it's possible to follow the course of the old line by taking the second roundabout exit - Lochat Road - which is closed to cars but walkers and cyclists are apparently permitted to use it. The road proceeds pleasantly enough through woodland adjoining Lodge Hill Camp, and swings eastwards at the end to reach Lodge Hill Lane. However, on reaching the lane you cannot continue eastwards along the course of the old line; the land is MOD-owned and unauthorised persons are not permitted. You would therefore have to bid a final farewell to the Chattenden & Upnor line which ended hereabouts, turn right here and walk all the way down Lodge Hill Lane, going forward into Chattenden Lane - a distance of well over a mile - and end up at the A228, only a fraction further on from the roundabout asterisked above. It is most frustrating. You could therefore choose to cut your losses, and rather than follow the old line from this roundabout via Lochat Road, take the last exit, Kitchener Road, and follow it briefly to a T-junction with Chattenden Lane, turning right to reach the A228. Cross the A228 to take advantage of the cycle path/footway on the other side, and proceed north-eastwards beside the A228 to the next roundabout. You're now able to walk along a road running parallel with the A228, the so-called Ratcliffe Highway, for over a mile. This involves quite a stiff climb but at the top of the hill there was at the time of writing a welcome pub/restaurant. The road emerges at Bell's Lane; turn left and go immediately over the roundabout into Dux Court Road.

If you've decided to give the Chattenden & Upnor line a miss, and you could be forgiven for doing so, your journey will start at Hoo St Werburgh, well served by buses from Rochester and Strood. From the crossroads in the village centre where Stoke Road, Main Road, Church Street and Bell's Lane meet, walk just west of north up Bell's Lane, swinging north-westwards to reach a roundabout junction with the A228. Cross straight over into Dux Court Road.

Walk down Dux Court Road, past the golf course entrance and woodland beyond, and just the other side of the woods, a little over a quarter of a mile from the roundabout, you'll see a gate and an MOD warning sign just to your left. Walk round the gate and follow the path beyond, and you'll soon reach a very forbidding gate with a roadway heading westwards (your left) on the other side. That is the course of the old line, a section of what was the Chattenden Naval Tramway. You can't join the old line just here, so return to the road and bear left, over what is marked by a road sign as a humpback bridge - actually the bridge over the old line and an adjacent stream. Look out very carefully for the humpback bridge sign facing the other way, and just beyond that scramble, at the first opportunity, through the thin vegetation into the field adjacent to the road to your right. Bear right and follow the right-hand field edge round the first corner, then (having walked parallel with the old line briefly) round the next

Trespassers not welcome - this section of the Chattenden Naval Tramway just east of Lodge Hill is quite definitely out of bounds!

corner; having done this, look for an opportunity to scramble through the vegetation into the next field, and do so. Bear right to follow the right-hand edge of the next field, going down to the corner then round so that you're once again parallel with the course of the old line. Now you need to keep your eyes open! Looking to your right, you'll see thick vegetation, but shortly before getting level with a prominent bush across the field to your left, you'll see the trees clear and get a good view to an orchard. It's at this point that you need to scramble down the bank, over a gully and through the undergrowth on the other side, and by veering left you'll find yourself looking down the course of the old line. It's not easy walking, this, but there are no manmade obstacles and you just need to be careful, watching where you are putting your feet! Your reward for this effort is a really lovely walk along the course of the old line in the shade of trees. The earlier slogging will all seem worthwhile! You emerge into the fields and arrive at a T-junction with a track at Solomon's Farm; turn right along the track - the old line made a rather smoother negotiation of this corner - and follow it back to the A228. Running parallel with your track is the extant Hoo Junction-Port Victoria line, a very pretty single track line at this point. Now you need to rejoin the old line at the point where it linked with the extant one. To do this, make your way up to the A228, cross it, then turn left to follow it uphill, in about 300 yards looking out carefully for and then following a very narrow signed footpath which goes off to the right, downhill, to reach the hamlet of Sharnal Street. Turn left to follow the road through the hamlet, then in roughly another 300 yards, before the roundabout at the end, turn right, south-eastwards, along a signed footpath. It appears to enter the back garden of a house, but follow the arrow carefully as you are directed eastwards across a field to a path junction with Roper's Green Lane.

Turn right to follow the lane south-westwards, and in just under half a mile you cross the single-track Hoo Junction-Port Victoria line again; immediately beyond the bridge crossing, turn hard left along a track which brings you down to, and follows eastwards parallel with, this line. Continue along the track which passes a hut, then enters rougher ground, and as you get level with a very prominent large bush in the field to the right, you will see a rough path leaving yours to head towards it. Follow this rough path to the bush, but do NOT be tempted to cross the ditch and go forward onto the better-defined path beyond; instead, staying to the left side of the ditch, follow the right-hand edge of the field, keeping the houses of the hamlet of Beluncle to your right. Although there is no trace of the old line at this point, you are effectively following it as it veered away from the extant Port Victoria line. The going is rough in places, and you should take care to avoid the risk of damage to crops, but eventually you arrive at a slip road* just beyond Beluncle Villas. Turn right to arrive at Stoke Road. Here the old line swung in a more south-easterly direction, heading across what is now a crop field towards what is now Kingsnorth Power Station. You may content yourself with tracing the course of the line with your eyes, following the road round (ignoring the turning off left to Stoke) past the fringes of the Kingsnorth Industrial Estate. Having negotiated a sharp right-hand bend and proceeded south-westwards, you reach an access road into the estate, which actually follows the course of the old line, but if you decide to take it you'll arrive at the perimeter of the power station and find you can go no further. The old line proceeded south-eastwards to a pier on the banks of the Medway, but it is now quite impossible to follow for its final stretch.

As if the demands of this walk were not enough, you now have another problem - getting back to civilisation. To do so, you have another choice. You could retrace your steps along the road to the slip road asterisked above but this time just keep going along Stoke Road, past the other buildings of Beluncle, and on to a sharp bend at Sturdee Cottages where the road swings right and uphill. Don't go right here but continue straight on along Stoke Road, just south of west, to the village of Hoo St Werburgh, just over 2 miles in total from the Kingsnorth complex. At Hoo St Werburgh there are refreshments and buses back to Strood and Rochester.

There is however a very energetic alternative, involving a link with the Stoke-Allhallows line described elsewhere in this book. Begin by following the road from the Kingsnorth complex back towards Beluncle, but at the very first left-hand bend (in just a few yards) leave the road by a service road that proceeds just east of north, keeping the buildings of the industrial estate to the right. The service road soon swings sharply right, and almost immediately beyond the bend, look for and follow a signed footpath going off to the left and proceed gently uphill over the extant Hoo Junction-Port Victoria line. Follow the path across a gentle hillside to a road in the hamlet of North Street. Turn right onto the road here and follow it initially south-eastwards, keeping to it as it swings sharply left and proceeds north-eastwards over a stream. Shortly you reach a crossroads junction with tracks, the left track going off to Tudor Farm, but you need to turn right, down to and over the railway crossing. Beyond the crossing, go forward to a clear green coastal path; turn left and follow what is a delightful path beside the Medway estuary with its vast number of little inlets, spits, salt marshes, pools and creeks. After a good two and a half miles, you find yourself immediately adjacent to the A228 on the east side of the villages of Stoke, Middle Stoke and (the largest) Lower Stoke. Drop down to the A228 using the gate and stile provided, and turn left to arrive shortly at the point where the extant Port Victoria railway crossed the A228. Go over the crossing and in a few yards, on the north side of the road, you'll be at the starting point for the Allhallows line walk.

WALK 3 - **ROCHESTER BRIDGE - CHATHAM CENTRAL**

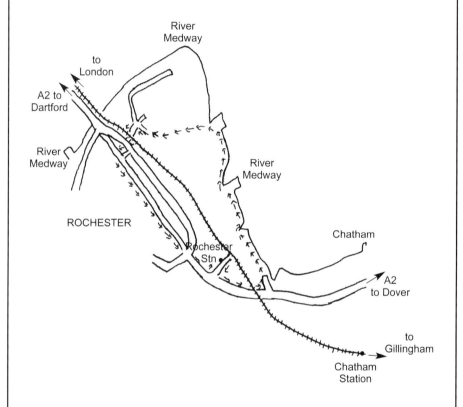

Scale: 8·4cm - 1km

WALK 3 - ROCHESTER BRIDGE - CHATHAM CENTRAL

Length:	2 miles round trip.
Start and Finish:	Rochester station.
Public Transport:	Regular trains serving Rochester on London Victoria-Sittingbourne-Faversham line.
Refreshments:	Rochester (P,C,S).
Conditions:	Although there are no traces of the old line, the terrain over which it crossed is easy to discern and it is a most pleasant walk, ideal for families and/or as a gentle afternoon stroll, with no obstructions and lots of things of interest. Be aware, though, that the riverside walk is advertised as "temporary;" the whole area is being developed in the next decade so the walk itself, or parts of it, may cease to be available.

History

The year 1860 saw the completion of a rail link between Faversham and London via Chatham by what had previously been the East Kent Railway, subsequently to become the London Chatham & Dover Railway (LCDR). Two years previously this company had also built a branch line from Chatham, on the east side of the Medway, to Strood on the west side. However the completion of the link to London led to a significant diminution in traffic on the Strood branch. Passenger services on that branch were effectively withdrawn and in fact the LCDR did provide a station on the west side of the Medway just beyond the Strood "spur," known as Rochester Bridge and ironically within very easy reach of the centre of Strood (this station shut in 1917). During the 1870's the Mayor of Rochester, Alderman Toomer, campaigned strongly for proper passenger services to Strood to be reinstated and in due course they were. However, the LCDR's great rival, the South Eastern Railway (SER) decided to build its own line, parallel to the LCDR one between Strood and Chatham via Rochester. Initially trains ran from Strood to a station called Rochester Common on the Chatham side of the Medway, this section of line opening in 1891, and the following year it was extended to a station called Chatham Central (which was in fact much nearer the centre of Rochester!). There were no other intermediate stations beside Rochester Common. From having an inadequate rail service between Strood and Chatham, the local populace therefore found itself with an excessive one, but unsurprisingly this absurd situation did not last long: the SER line shut in 1911, although ironically part of the spur between Strood and the Medway bridge on the SER line was adopted by the Strood-Chatham line which remained. There is now absolutely no evidence on the ground that the SER's superfluous line ever existed, and in the next decade the course of the line will undergo a further radical transformation(see below).

Walking the Line

Make your way out of the main entrance of Rochester station and walk along the station approach road. Turn left at the end and walk along what is quite a busy street, soon passing under the existing railway, then shortly beyond the overbridge, bear hard left into Doust Way. Follow Doust Way to its end, keeping a car park to your left. Just to your right here are new flats which have been built on the site of Chatham Central station on the old line; note that you're a lot closer to Rochester than Chatham and actually nowhere near the centre of Chatham!! Now go forward through gates to join the brand new riverside path and simply follow the path beside the Medway, keeping it to your right and enjoying excellent views out to the Medway, back to Chatham behind you, and Rochester to the left. This is a lovely riverside walk, and although there are no traces of the old line to be seen, you can follow the course of it with your eyes, as it passed across the middle of the grassy area separating you on your riverside walk from the still extant railway line. You can see how astonishingly useless the old line really

Looking towards Chatham across land along which the Rochester Bridge-Chatham Central line ran - ending nowhere near the centre of Chatham!

was! Note that there are big plans for this grassy area and you'll see numerous information boards providing more details about this; essentially it will be very heavily developed with houses, shops, open spaces and other amenities, albeit the project won't be finished till 2022. Your riverside walk ends when the concrete path gives out and you go forward along rougher ground to metal exit gates and a junction with Gas House Lane, the site of the one intermediate station called Rochester Common. Look straight ahead to see the course of the old line across what is now a car park, going forward to link with the extant line at the Medway bridge crossing. Now turn left into Gas House Lane, go under the extant line, and turn left immediately beyond, then cross the road and take the first right turning into Northgate. This takes you to Rochester's lovely main street, with its castle, cathedral and multiplicity of tempting pubs, restaurants and cafes. To get back to the station, turn left along the street and follow it to its end, going forward to cross over the road and continuing straight on to arrive shortly back at the station approach road.

WALK 4 - **STOKE - ALLHALLOWS**

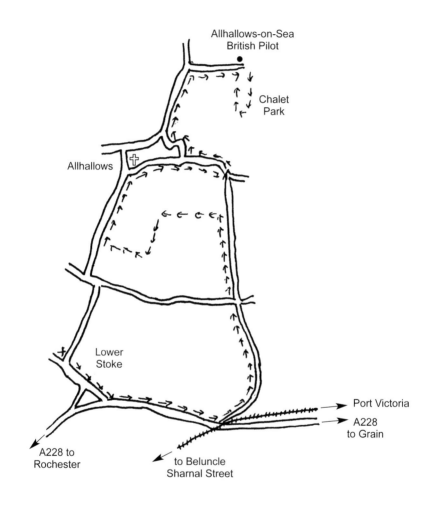

Scale: 4·2cm - 1km

WALK 4 - **STOKE - ALLHALLOWS**

Length:	5 miles.
Start:	Lower Stoke.
Finish:	Allhallows-on-Sea.
Public Transport:	Regular buses (ARR) serving Lower Stoke and Allhallows-on-Sea on Chatham-Grain route.
Refreshments:	Lower Stoke (P,S); Allhallows-on-Sea (P,S).
Conditions:	Despite the distance from start to finish as the crow flies being so short - less than 2 miles - and some good sections of old line being available for walking, there is of necessity a lot of backtracking involved which makes this walk longer than one feels it really needs to be. However the scenery is fascinating throughout, there are no real demands on the walker, and even with the backtracking it is comfortably manageable in half a day.

History

The line from Stoke to Allhallows was a branch line off the rail route, opened in 1882, linking the main London-Gravesend-Strood-Rochester line at Hoo Junction with Port Victoria at the south-eastern end of the Isle of Grain. It had been hoped that Port Victoria would develop into a major continental sea port, and indeed it was possible for passengers to catch a steamer from Port Victoria across the Medway to Sheerness with connections there for Folkestone and the Continent. However, Port Victoria did not develop as hoped, and during the 1920's alternative means of increasing revenue from the line were sought. Southern Railway(SR), who were by this time responsible for the Hoo Junction-Port Victoria route, decided to seek authorisation to build a branch from a point on this route between Middle Stoke and Grain Crossing to Allhallows which had been identified as a feasible location for a new seaside resort in north Kent. The railway company actually acquired a financial interest in the Allhallows-on-Sea Estate Company which intended to transform the village and its surrounding featureless marshland into that new resort. The new company in return donated land for use as a railway and also provided some of the finance.

In June 1929 the necessary authorisation was given, and work started on the 1.75 mile branch in August 1931. There were no construction difficulties, the line passing through

Full steam ahead - an easily followable section of the Stoke-Allhallows line.

low-lying pasture fields and ditches which necessitated the construction of a number of culverts. The single-track line opened on 14 May 1932 when 700 travellers arrived at Allhallows by special train from London, and to coincide with the line's opening, halts on the Hoo Junction-Port Victoria route were upgraded. In the line's early days, there were actually daily direct services from Allhallows to Charing Cross, presumably intended to show how commuters might make use of the line, but these were discontinued within a few months. The line was, however, very popular with day trippers, and on Sundays in summer 1934 over 72,000 journeys were made, with 9,500 journeys made on a single Sunday in August 1934. As a result the branch line was doubled and Allhallows station was extended with goods facilities available. By 1939 between 10 and 12 trains ran each weekday from Gravesend with 7 on Sundays, rising to 13 on Sundays during the high season, and this marked the zenith in the line's popularity. During the austere post-Second World War years, passenger numbers fell dramatically; Allhallows never developed into the resort it was hoped it would (not helped by the fact that SR declined to electrify the line), and the line's fortunes weren't helped by SR's successor British Rail's decision to deploy noisy and uncomfortable diesel railcars on the branch. Although in the mid-1950's the frequency of services was similar to that of the late 1930's, winter trains were hardly used, and in 1957 the branch was reduced to single track. In 1959 the line was again excluded from the electrification programme for railways in North Kent. With passenger numbers continuing to decline, British Rail applied to close the line and despite stiff opposition passenger services ceased on Sunday 3 December 1961 goods services having ceased on the previous day. Passenger services on the "main" route from Hoo Junction(the terminus of which was now called

"Grain") also ceased on 3 December 1961, but freight services continued and are still running today; Grain remains an active terminal as the forwarding point for granite shipped from Scotland.

Walking the Line

It must be emphasized that the whole of the walk along the course of the old line as far as the + symbol below is on private tracks and paths with no public rights of way. Please refer to my introductory notes.

The walk starts in the village of Lower Stoke. From the road junction in the very centre of the village follow the road just south of east out of the village to a T-junction with the A228 Grain road; turn left onto it and follow it for about half a mile to just short of the level crossing with the Hoo Junction-Port Victoria railway. About 25 yards before the crossing, turn left onto a gated dirt track. Pass through the gate and follow the track, veering gently left to cross over a hump bridge and proceed along the track between areas of marshland, shortly arriving at a junction of tracks. Ignore the ones going hard left and forking right, but go straight ahead through a gate (there may be a side one open) veering just west of north and following a very obvious path. You are now on the course of the old line. Continue under the pylon lines and keep along the track through attractive open countryside, passing over a channel where you may get some entertainment in the form of flocks of birds skimming the surface of the water. You veer very gently northwards, the buildings of Allhallows clearly visible ahead, and on a clear day you can see the buildings of Southend across the Thames. Unfortunately your progress is halted by some insurmountable fencing+. You need to bear left and follow the right-hand field edge, and shortly are forced south-westwards, away from your objective, keeping a channel to your right. Ahead of you and just to the right is the big barn of Nord Farm; about 150 yards short of the barn, look out for a plank bridge over the channel to the right. Turn right to cross the bridge and continue straight on uphill on a right-hand field edge to arrive at a T-junction with a road. Turn right to follow the road, passing the Chimnies Rest Home and proceeding to the inland village centre of Allhallows. Immediately before the pretty church, bear right along Binney Road and follow this road downhill, veering sharp left and then right to pull away from the houses, the road becoming a track. On reaching the valley floor, you arrive at a green area where horses are kept, and you'll see a gate on your right stating "Enter At Your Own Risk." This brings you back onto the course of the old line which you can follow briefly back towards the fencing that barred your progress before! Return to the track continuation of Binney Road*. Now looking ahead you can see the course of the old line which despite being shown on maps as a public footpath is now definitely not; it is heavily fenced and used as a horse enclosure. Beyond, you should be able to make out a stout fence and then the start of a large caravan park. Forward access is, unfortunately, obstructed and you will need to backtrack.

There are two possibilities now. The recommended route is as follows. Retrace your

The Stoke-Allhallows line, the broad open countryside contrasting with the sprawl of housing behind.

steps along Binney Road but take the first right turn into St David's Road and follow it up to a T-junction with Avery Way. There's a useful parade of shops just to your left here at the T-junction. Turn right to follow Avery Way uphill, then turn sharp right at the top, not going forward into the holiday park, and walk quite steeply downhill along Avery Way, eastwards, to pass the British Pilot pub which is to your left, and a big chalet park to your right. Don't veer left but go straight on through a small car park to reach a locked gate - in fact you can easily walk round the side of it. Bear right to walk southwards along a wide green strip, keeping the backs of the chalets to your right and enjoying extensive views to your left which on a clear day include Grain, the Isle of Sheppey, the confluence of the Medway and the Thames, and the buildings of Southend-on-Sea! As you reach the far end of this strip you can look southwards back along the course of the old line. At the time of writing it was possible to lift the barbed wire fencing to the left to give access to an adjacent field giving a better view, but this is not recommended - see my introductory notes. From the green strip you've been following, bear right at the far end to access the main chalet park road and follow it northwards, now actually on the course of the old line once more**. The approach road veers right at the end to arrive back at Avery Way with the British Pilot opposite, this junction beside what was the end of the line. There are buses available from here back to Strood, Rochester and Chatham.

There is a possible (shorter) alternative. From the point single-asterisked above turn back briefly, but instead of backtracking along Binney Road to St David's Road you may be able to turn right along the right-hand field edge parallel with the old line. This field may be overgrown, thus ruling it out, but if you can negotiate it, follow the field edge up to the top corner, veer round and then, as soon as you can, scramble over the field boundary to arrive at the edge of a par 3 golf course. Turn sharp right along the right-hand edge to the corner, where there's a gap in the fencing. Pass through the gap to find yourself at the southern end of the main chalet park road; turn left and follow it northwards, on the course of the old line once more, then follow instructions from the point double-asterisked above. It's worth turning right when you get to Avery Way, following the road to its very end to enjoy the views across the Thames Estuary.

Passengers outnumbered by sheep on the Stoke-Allhallows line

WALK 5 - ISLE OF SHEPPEY

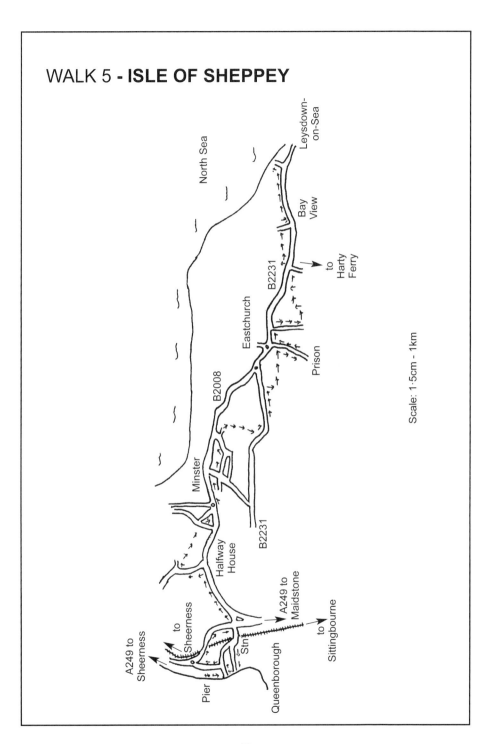

North Sea

Leysdown-on-Sea

Bay View

to Harty Ferry

B2231

Eastchurch

Prison

B2008

Minster

B2231

Halfway House

A249 to Maidstone

to Sittingbourne

A249 to Sheerness

to Sheerness

Stn

Pier

Queenborough

Scale: 1·5cm - 1km

WALK 5 - ISLE OF SHEPPEY

Length:	11 miles, to include branch as described.
Start:	Queenborough station.
Finish:	Leysdown-on-Sea (hereinafter Leysdown).
Public Transport:	Regular trains serving Queenborough and Sheerness on Sittingbourne-Sheerness line; regular buses(ARR) from Leysdown to Sheerness.
Refreshments:	Queenborough (P,S); Halfway Houses (P,S,C); Minster (P,S); Eastchurch (P,S); Leysdown (P,S,C)
Conditions:	There are two walks here, as it were, for the price of one: to start with, the Queenborough-Queenborough Dock branch off the still extant Sittingbourne-Sheerness line, then a much longer walk exploring the course of the Sheppey Light Railway between Queenborough and Leysdown. It makes for a long day's walk and is a classic curate's egg - good in parts. There is some excellent old line walking available, particularly between Halfway Houses and Minster and between New Rides and Old Rides, and there are some other sections where the old line can be clearly discerned. However there is also of necessity some very tedious road walking, and the final section between Bay View and Leysdown is a real anticlimax.

History

Sheerness on the Isle of Sheppey, very much part of Kent both then and now, was reached by a 7-mile single-track branch from the main London-Rochester-Faversham line at Sittingbourne which opened in July 1860. It remains a busy line to this day, but travellers along it may not realise there are a number of branches off it. One was very near the terminus of the still extant line at Sheerness. Whereas nowadays trains veer north-eastwards to arrive at the terminus, trains previously ran straight on to a station a little to the west of the existing one; it was originally called Sheerness but renamed Sheerness Dockyard when the present station opened in 1883. Trains then called at both stations, having to reverse out of one to get to the other, but in 1922 a spur was built which bypassed the Dockyard station and this led to the closure of the Dockyard

A rare section of walkable line between Queenborough and Leysdown on the Isle of Sheppey, just north-east of Queenborough.

station to passenger traffic. However what is now effectively a branch line from the extant railway towards the site of the old Dockyard station is still used by the steel works that is there now, and the extension into the docks is also sometimes used, so this "branch" is outside the scope of this book. Another branch, now defunct, consisted of a short piece of line from one of the intermediate stations, Queenborough (the last before Sheerness). This branch was opened in May 1876 to reach Queenborough Pier subsequent to an agreement with the Zealand Shipping Company to transfer the Ramsgate terminal of its ferry link with the Netherlands to this pier. Just six years later the pier caught fire leading to the transfer of the terminal to Dover; the pier was rebuilt but unbelievably was destroyed by another fire in 1900! Once more it was rebuilt but closed following the outbreak of World War 1 and never saw regular use again. The branch line subsequently remained open for freight but was very rarely used and it is surprising that it took till as long as 1956 for it to close altogether.

And so to the third and most significant branch. The Sittingbourne-Sheerness line hugged the west coast of Sheppey leaving much of the island remote from the railway. In acknowledgement of this a line linking Queenborough with Leysdown-on-Sea, at the far eastern end of the island, was proposed. In April 1899 an Order was granted for the construction of this line, to be called the Sheppey Light Railway, and it was duly opened in August 1901, absorbed by the London Chatham & Dover Railway just four years later. It was built by the famous railway entrepreneur Colonel Stephens, and typical of his "shoestring" railways, was very economical in construction with very basic stations, no earthworks, no signals at intermediate stations, no bridges, and a number of level crossings, some ungated. There was an overall speed limit of just 25mph, and with several intermediate stops - Sheerness East, East Minster-on-Sea, Minster-on-Sea, Brambledown Halt, Eastchurch and Harty Road Halt - journeys must have seemed painfully slow. An average journey took about 35 minutes; the 6.45am from Queenborough in 1922, calling at all stations, reached Leysdown at 7.25am. At 40 minutes for less than nine miles, cycling it would have been quicker for many. Passenger services were very infrequent, with just 6 round trips a day in 1922 on Mondays to Fridays, and only 4 in 1948. Minster and Leysdown, the two major settlements served by the line, failed to generate sufficient passenger traffic, ambitious development schemes which would have attracted more passengers came to nothing, and holidaymakers coming to the area were tending to do so by road. The end was inevitable and the line closed to both passengers and freight in 1950.

Walking the Line

The walk incorporates the branch to Queenborough Pier, and the much longer walk to Leysdown. From Queenborough station, walk up to Main Road and head westwards towards the waterfront, very soon bearing left into High Street and in fact following it to the waterside. Bear right to follow the concrete promenade, getting fine views across to Grain Power Station; continue all the way along the promenade until it swings sharply right, away from the water, the views here stretching northwards to Southend across the Thames. Immediately beyond where the path swings right is the site of Queenborough Pier station. The path, going "inland," soon crosses the course of the old line heading south-eastwards, but its course either side is impossible to discern. Retrace your steps along the promenade but turn left before High Street into North Road and follow it to where the B2007 Whiteway Road goes off to the left. Now follow Whiteway Road fractionally west of north, to a point shortly before a sharp right bend, where a concrete road leading into an industrial estate goes off to the left. Immediately opposite, to the right, is a wire gate beyond which you can see another gate; this is the course of the old Queenborough Pier branch, but it is impossible to follow. Return to Whiteway Road and continue along it to arrive at a roundabout junction with the A249. Turn right to follow alongside it, keeping to the right (west) side - fortunately there is room for pedestrians as this is a very busy road. Looking right, as you approach the bridge crossing over the extant Sittingbourne-Sheerness railway line, you can see the old Queenborough Pier branch, with a length of track still in situ. Now descend from the bridge crossing, and roughly halfway between the crossing and a sharp right-hand bend of the A249 look out for a path leading off to the right heading for modern housing. Turn right to follow this path - it is in fact the course of the old Leysdown line, just beyond its branching off from the main Sheerness line. The "join" is now covered by new housing development, and when you reach this development you're forced back to the A249 on the same path, albeit now heading in the right direction! Beyond the A249 you'll see that the course of the old line, clearly delineated and followable with the eyes as it heads north-east across the marsh, is quite impossible to access, so bear right to follow alongside the A249 south-eastwards to a major junction, and here turn left to follow beside the A250 Queenborough Road to arrive at Halfway Houses. There's an excellent range of amenities here - do take advantage! You come to a significant road junction here, with the A250 Halfway Road heading left (north-westwards) here towards Sheerness, and you need to take this road. You reach a sharp left bend and mini-roundabout; just before it, look to the left to see the course of the old line coming in from the left (but still inaccessible). Actually on the mini-roundabout, turn right into Power Station Road, passing the site of Sheerness East station which was just beside this junction. Power Station Road is pleasanter than it sounds, even more so when as you progress along it there's a parallel strip of green to the right, a public amenity which is actually the course of the old line. Just beyond this parallel strip, as you approach the golf club car park, look out for a gate to the right; by opening this gate you'll find you can join and follow the old line as it continues to run parallel with the road. However you're forced back by the vegetation and need to join the road again, which you follow past the golf club car park to reach a gate where the road effectively becomes a rough track. Bear right just before the gate to join a path which immediately swings left and now proceeds delightfully south-eastwards along the course of the old line providing lovely walking, the highlight of the whole journey to Leysdown. Sadly when the path arrives at Scrapsgate Road you're forced off the old line again; bear right here and first left into Sunnyside Avenue, the houses to the left separating you from the course of the old line with which you're now running parallel. You reach a T-junction with the busy B2008 Minster Road. Cross it and turn left to follow it, the green in front of the pub just beyond Fleetwood Close marking the point where the old line crossed the road, the old East Minster-on-Sea station (actually some distance from the sea, and west of the village of Minster!!) on the north-west side of the road at this point. Pass the pub then bear right onto a footpath immediately opposite house number 294, the path going forward to the bottom(western) end of Blatcher Close; turn left to follow Blatcher Close south-eastwards, keeping an electricity works to the right. By following the right side of the works perimeter fence you'll be back on the course of the old line, but again the vegetation beats you back and you now need to contine along Blatcher Close to its end, going straight on into Harps Avenue and proceeding along this undistinguished road, the houses on the right separating you from the course of the old line.

You arrive at a T-junction with Scocles Road; by turning right and following the road just past the houses, you'll reach the course of the old line where it crossed Scocles Road - the site of another halt, called Minster-on-Sea - but there's no trace of the line or platform here and no way onto the course of the old line. Walk very briefly back up Scocles Road and turn right into Drake Avenue which you follow south-eastwards, with housing development to your right separating you from the course of the old line. Turn right at the end of Drake Avenue onto Elm Lane, then turn almost immediately left, just before a sharp right-hand bend, onto a driveway that takes you towards Sheppey Light Farm. This is significant in that you're back on the course of the old line again and the farm's name is obviously inspired by the old line, with a picture of a locomotive on the farm gate. On reaching the farm gate you can go no further, so retrace your steps to Elm Lane and turn right to follow it uphill. As the road swings to the left, turn right onto the Tadwell Farm approach road, looking out for and crossing a stile on the right soon after joining the approach road. Now aim for another stile situated diagonally left across the field, and having crossed the second stile continue in the same direction along a very ill-defined path, going over the crest of a hill and then going forward to a gate at the (fenced) east side of the field. Bear right to pass through the gate and now head just west of south along what is a good clear path with superb views across Sheppey, the

A glorious spring morning on the course of the Queenborough-Leysdown line between Halfway Houses and Minster.

Swale and the north Kent countryside. You pass just to the right of the Brambledown Farm buildings and arrive at a track; go forward to follow the track downhill, crossing the course of the old line and arriving at the B2231.

Turn left to walk alongside the B2231, a very busy road for a "B" road with no pavement, and almost immediately you pass the site of Brambledown Halt (which is to the left), where the old line crossed this road. Shortly you reach a road leading to New Hook Farm on the right; if you walk down this road, you will almost immediately reach the

The line between Queenborough and Leysdown becomes harder to follow the nearer you reach Leysdown - this is a rather sorry section, albeit technically accessible for walkers, between the Harty Ferry turning and Bay View. Note the parked vehicle!

point where the old line crossed it, now heading south-east away from the B2231, but its course is completely obliterated by the crops. Look half-left and you will see the rather formidable buildings and fences of Stanford Hill Prison, the line in fact passing just below the hill on this side. This gives you an idea of the course it would have taken as far as Church Road which is also the Stanford Hill Prison approach road. Return to the B2231 and now plod along it in an easterly direction, passing the approach road for Old Hook Farm; the old line crossed this approach road, but there's little point in following it as there's no trace of the line at all. However you should take the next track turning to the right, signed Groves Farm. Follow this past Newbuildings Cottages on the hillside and drop down to the foot of the hill, where going off to the left is a metalled lane which you need to follow; it isn't even on maps and isn't a designated public right of way, so please refer to my introductory notes. The track runs roughly parallel with the course of the old line - this being a little way to the south, very approximately halfway between you and the prominent hillside on which the prison is built - and rises gently to pass through the Parsonage Farm buildings and arrive at Church Road.

Turn right to follow Church Road south-westwards for just under a third of a mile from the top of the Parsonage Farm approach road towards the prison complex, passing the left turn into Kent View Drive and, shortly afterwards and also on the left, Stanbourne House. You're now by the site of the old Eastchurch station, which was on the west side of Church Road here. Immediately beyond the house is a gate, and by surmounting this (please refer to my introductory notes) you can briefly follow the course of the old line through quite thick vegetation, until your way forward is blocked by wooden fencing topped with barbed wire, and disappointingly you'll need to backtrack. Turn right to follow Church Road up to the roundabout junction with Rowetts Way. The village of Eastchurch is just over the other side, if you require refreshment; however, your route turns right to follow the B2231 (effectively a bypass for Eastchurch) steadily uphill, although there is a wide grass verge so the walking is not unpleasant. Shortly a road comes in from the left, and opposite, to your right, is a lane heading just east of south, the New Rides approach road. Turn right to follow this road which is signed as private but there are no obstructions to access, so please refer to my introductory notes. On a clear day the views from here will be magnificent, extending right out to sea and including the spectacular twin towers of Reculver to the east of Herne Bay much further along the Kent coast.

The road begins to dip down; you pass New Rides Bungalow which is to your left, and soon you arrive at another house just to your right, the topmost building of the main New Rides complex. By turning right along the left-hand edge of the field directly above the house, you can briefly follow the old line back towards the old Eastchurch station, but you soon find yourself in impenetrable vegetation and you're forced to backtrack. Return to the New Rides approach road but this time cross straight over and you're now able to follow what is quite a well-defined and easily negotiated section of old line, heading towards Old Rides Farm. You come to a field boundary which is quite thick with vegetation but by looking carefully you'll see there's a stile which you can use to cross into the next field; here you need to bear left, briefly away from the course of the old line, along a clear track by the left-hand field edge. The track now heads northwards and bends sharply to reach a T-junction with another track onto which you turn right, then bear immediately right again to resume a course just north of east, heading for Old Rides Farm. As you progress you will in fact be briefly back on the course of the old line. Don't enter the farm complex but veer round to the left of it, aiming for the metalled approach road coming in from the B2231. Now swinging away from the course of the old line, which crossed the B2231 just by the junction with Harty Ferry Road a little further on, you go forward to the Old Rides Farm approach road and turn left to follow it back to the B2231. Turn right to follow the main road to the junction with Harty Ferry Road just under half a mile further on, the old line followable with the eyes through the fields to your right.

At the junction of the B2231 with Harty Ferry Road - there was a halt here called Harty Road - bear left as shown by a public footpath sign. At the very start of the footpath on the right you'll see some crude fencing beyond which the old line can be observed heading eastwards, fairly well-defined at this point. Just walk a little way past this fencing and bear right to walk parallel with the old line on its north side. It may be possible for you to get onto the line in one or two places, but you won't be able to stay on it! Continuing eastwards, you proceed along a right-hand field edge, keeping the course of the old line to your right, now approaching the village of Bay View. You need to look out carefully for a very prominent wooden building backing onto the course of the old line; having passed just beyond that building, watch for a gate in the fencing to your right, which you need to pass through, crossing over a ditch and entering a field. Now bear left to follow the field eastwards, keeping the course of the old line to the right as it proceeds through the back gardens of houses in Bay View. You come to a very prominent round building shaped like a semi-circle; pass to the left of that, then veer right and walk along the right-hand edge of the grassy area to a double gate, passing through the gate to arrive in Mustards Road. NOTE: The section of walk from the semi-circular building to the double gate involves walking round the edge of part of the garden of a property called The Chase in Mustards Road. It is essential you seek permission before entering it.

It is impossible to make further progress along the old line, so turn right to follow Mustards Road to its junction with the B2231 - there's a useful pub just by the junction - and now turn left to follow the B2231 towards Leysdown. Plod on along the B2231, there being frankly little point in taking any of the roads going off to the left; once Bay View has passed but before reaching Leysdown, the houses relent to allow you to see the course the line would have taken, along the bottom of the little valley and into what is now a vast amalgam of holiday camps, built without too much respect for old railway aficionados. Soon you reach the centre of Leysdown with its mass of shops, cafes and amusement arcades, best visited outside busy holiday periods. By turning left into

The Promenade you will, just before its end, arrive at where the line itself ended, but there's no trace whatsoever of its existence now, and it's all a rather sad anticlimax. The only consolation is that there will be no shortage of places to enjoy a cup of tea or maybe something stronger before returning to Sheerness on the bus.

WALK 6 - **FAVERSHAM QUAY**

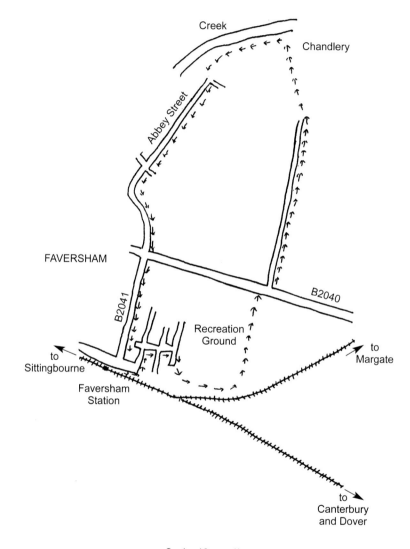

Scale: 10cm - 1km

WALK 6 - **FAVERSHAM QUAY**

Length:	2.5 miles.
Start and Finish:	Faversham station.
Public Transport:	Regular trains serving Faversham on London-Chatham-Canterbury-Dover/Ramsgate route.
Refreshments:	Faversham (P,C,S).
Conditions:	A very straightforward and rewarding walk which can easily be accomplished in little more than an hour. Faversham is a most attractive town in its own right and you should make time to explore it before or after your walk.

(This is, with due respect to H.P. White, a somewhat surprising line to find included in his Gazetteer. It was a freight-only line, on the face of it no more remarkable than many other non-passenger lines in Kent which do NOT feature in the Gazetteer, with no plans to make it available for passenger use and not featuring at all on a number of maps showing past and present Kent railway lines. However, it is a good representative example of one of many freight lines branching off existing lines in Kent, and even if you find the walk uninspiring in places, you can at least enjoy Faversham!)

History

1853 saw the inception of the East Kent Railway(EKR), later to become the London Chatham & Dover Railway(LCDR) and in January 1858 the EKR opened a line linking Chatham, already served by rail, with the then busy port of Faversham. Authorisation had also been given for the company to build a branch to Faversham Quay, beside the creek linking the town with the north Kent coast. This branch opened in April 1860 but for the purposes of carrying freight only, and remained open until 1964; among the businesses it served was the United Fertilisers warehouse which still stands today. Despite the fact that it closed nearly half a century ago, there is a surprising amount of evidence of the old line still remaining.

Walking the Line

Turn right out of the main station entrance and walk along Station Road, passing but not turning into Newton Road. At the far end of Station Road turn sharp left into St

Mary's Road then very shortly right into Chapel Street, going forward into Preston Place to arrive at a T-junction with Park Road, a recreation ground ahead of you. Turn right to follow Park Road southwards, then keeping a car park to your right, go forward beyond Park Road onto a concrete cycle path which rises onto an embankment above the recreation ground. Very soon you'll see the railway on your right, and reach the point where the old line met the existing one. Now the cycle path on its embankment swings round to the left(northwards) and you will clearly see the old line running parallel with the cycle path but separated from you by a tall metalled fence with no chance whatsoever of accessing it. The closest you can get to it is by way of a bridge which goes

across the old line into an industrial estate. Continue along the cycle path to its end at a T-junction with Whitstable Road, noting the embankment of the old line which is very obvious to the right. Turn right and then immediately left into Abbey Fields and follow it, the old line now obliterated by the houses of Abbey Fields to your left. Beyond the houses there's a sign saying there's no public right of way beyond, but access appears to be no problem, so continue in the same direction, the course of the old line parallel with you to your left.

You reach a point* where the metalled lane veers half-left, with a sign indicating this is the way to the chandlery and only authorised persons are permitted. However at the time of writing access did not appear to present a problem and indeed as you walk on down to the chandlery and the waters of the creek, you will arrive at the course of

Trees now grace the top of the embankment followed by the little Faversham Quay branch.

the Saxon Shore Way close to the water's edge. Turn left to walk along the left bank of the creek, following the course of the old line as far as its end just before the very imposing United Fertilisers building. Simply now continue beyond the building on the course of the well-signposted Saxon Shore Way; when you reach the black weatherboarded boatyard buildings go to the landward side of them, then follow what is a metalled road, veering left and then almost immediately right to the end of the very attractive Abbey Street. Follow it to the centre of Faversham. To return to the station, continue into Court Street, turn almost immediately left into Crescent Road past the superstore, then go forward into Newton Road. Follow this to the end and you'll find yourself back at Station Road, close to the station where you began.

If for whatever reason you're unable to continue to the creek from the point asterisked above, retrace your steps via Abbey Fields to Whitstable Road, turn right and follow the road forward to East Street; at the T-junction, turn right and follow Crescent Road round past the superstore, bearing right into Court Street and going straight on into Abbey Street. At the very end bear left then almost immediately right and follow the metalled lane down to the creek side, continuing as signposted along the Saxon Shore Way past the United Fertilisers building. The old line continued along the creekside before swinging inland back towards Abbey Fields through the chandlery.

WALK 7 - **WESTERHAM - DUNTON GREEN**

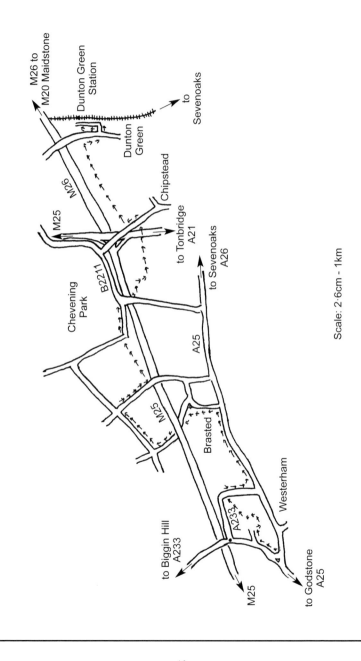

WALK 7 - **WESTERHAM - DUNTON GREEN**

Length:	6 miles.
Start:	Westerham.
Finish:	Dunton Green.
Public Transport:	Regular buses (ARR) serving Westerham from Sevenoaks; regular trains serving Dunton Green on Sevenoaks-London Charing Cross route.
Refreshments:	Westerham (P,S,C); Brasted (P); Dunton Green (P,S).
Conditions:	This is a walk of three parts: the first part, a very pleasant and interesting walk along a good section of old line; the second part, involving necessary but not too unpleasant road walking; and to finish, a really splendid walk along the old line. The noise of the M25, which has swallowed up the middle part of the line, is never far away but this is in fact a pleasant and interesting walk in very attractive North Downs scenery, and manageable in half a day.

History

The branch line sprang from a desire by local people to connect the town of Westerham, left aside by the mid-19th century boom in building railways, with the main network. It was local enterprise, motivated by concern for the general economic development of the area, that promoted the scheme, known as the Westerham Valley Railway; work began in October 1879 and the single-track line opened on 7th July 1881. Between Dunton Green, where the branch left the main line, and Westerham, its terminus, there was just one intermediate station, at Brasted, and an unstaffed halt called Chevening Halt which did not actually open until 1906 and which consisted of a single platform. When services began there were 11 trains each way on weekdays, and 8 on Sundays. In the mid-1920's there were 16 weekday departures from Westerham with an extra trip on three weekdays, and 10 Sunday departures; by 1952 this had risen to 22 weekday and 15 Sunday departures. However, whilst at this stage the line was well used by commuters, off-peak traffic was very light, and there was an additional problem in that with the discontinuance of steam trains on the Southern Region it was difficult to provide suitable alternative rolling stock. It was decided to close the line, and although the Transport Users Consultative Committee recommended against closure, they were

The Westerham-Dunton Green line emerging from Westerham - note the spire of Westerham church in the background

overruled by the then Minister of Transport, Ernest Marples, who when challenged in Parliament claimed that the line was losing £26,000 per annum. The line was shut at the end of October 1961. Attempts were subsequently made by a newly-formed Westerham Valley Railway Association to run trains independently, but unfortunately this coincided with plans for the M25, Kent County Council saying the Association could only keep the line if they paid over £25,000 for a bridge to carry the M25 over the track - something they could not do. Now, ironically, the M25 covers much of the old trackbed.

Walking the Line
Starting from the delightful square in the centre of Westerham, turn north into London Road and follow it past the right turns of Holcombe Close and Quebec Avenue, soon reaching a junction with Hortons Way. Turn right to follow this road, and very soon there's a left turn into an industrial estate along The Flyers Way; signs warn there's no public right of way here, but if you decide to follow it (please refer to my introductory notes) to its end, you'll reach a raised grassy embankment with a tall fence behind. This is the course of the old line, and by backtracking - you have no choice but to backtrack! - you can see how the line finished, a large industrial unit now covering the course it would have taken to reach the old station (now completely obliterated) by the junction of Hortons Way and London Road. Now follow Hortons Way eastwards to just short of Railway Terrace, a charming little narrow street with a nice pictorial street sign - a very

apposite name with the old line once running past its top end. However a little before the Railway Terrace turning, bear right to enter a sports field. Almost immediately bear left to follow the left-hand field edge round, bearing right at the first corner and following about halfway to the next corner, but then turning left to cross a bridge over a stream and then immediately left along a field-edge path towards houses, going parallel with the stream. As the path swings right(north-east), you're now on the course of the old line; look left to see how the old line ran along the backs of the houses. Now proceed north-eastwards alongside the houses, on the field-edge path and then forward across an open field, enjoying lovely views ahead and also back to Westerham and its church. You arrive at a gate and junction with the A233; at the time of writing this gate was locked but the maps clearly show a right of way over it.

Cross the road* and turn right then immediately bear left as signed via a stile onto a track going

Looking eastwards from Westerham on the Dunton Green line. This peaceful scene belies the fact that the M25 is barely half a mile east of this point.

The old station house at Brasted close to the Westerham-Dunton Green line. The station itself has been demolished and the old line is now part of the M25

uphill to a hump-back bridge over the M25. Just before the bridge, bear right into the field and bear half-right to follow parallel with the hedge, the course of the old railway effectively traced by this hedge, until a fence bars your way. The line cannot now be followed between here and Chevening, for the very simple reason that the M25 has

Stretching ahead - two views of an excellent section of the Westerham-Dunton Green line near Chevening, on a rather soggy March morning.

been built along its course! Retrace your steps to the spot asterisked above, and bear left to follow the A233 just east of south, then close to the junction of the A233 with the A25, bear left onto a signed footpath which heads a little north of east across a field and goes forward to a footbridge across a stream. Cross this then swing sharp right to cross a second footbridge, follow the path across a field to arrive at the A25, and bear left now to follow the A25 for just under a mile as far as Brasted. On arrival in the village, bear left up Church Road, and as you arrive at the church, bear left to follow a signed footpath through the churchyard, keeping the church to your right. Beyond the churchyard, go forward to the road again, at this point named Station Road. Ahead of you is a tunnel under the M25; just before the tunnel you can turn right to follow a slip road leading up to the M25, the top of the slip road coinciding with the site of Brasted station, and by looking to the right you can see the old stationmaster's house which still stands. However obviously there's no chance of following the old line, so go back down the slip road, bear right to walk under the tunnel, and follow the road, now Hogtrough Hill, north-westwards and uphill to a crossroads. Bear right here and follow the road, enjoying super views to the North Downs to the left, and a huge swathe of countryside to the right, including of course the M25, the route of which at least enables you to follow the line with your eyes! Take the next road turning to your right, effectively a staggered crossroads junction, and walk downhill along Brasted Hill Road back towards the M25. As you approach the M25, look out carefully for a signed footpath going to the left; bear left along the footpath, going forward, just north of east, to farm buildings, turning right at a T-junction with a farm road and right at the next T-junction with Ovenden Road. Follow this road which heads for the M25, then swings left to go parallel with it, and arrives at another T-junction, this time with the B2211. Turn right onto the B2211 to cross over the M25, looking left as you get over the other side in order to follow the continuation of the old line with your eyes; the old line veers away to the right+ just here, but it's still totally inaccessible.

Walk a little way beyond the bridge, and very shortly turn left onto a signed path down a very steep bank to a field. Follow the left-hand field edge, keeping a ditch to your left, veering round to the right and then shortly walking through a gap in the vegetation to the left; cross the ditch and bear right to follow the right-hand edge of a field(the ditch to your right), now walking down towards a lake. You reach some new fencing where you turn left and walk along a right-hand field edge, with lakes down to your right. Go forward to follow a green path past farm buildings and on to a metalled lane which you follow across the M25/A21 link motorway downhill to a junction with Chevening Road. Turn left up the road past Chevening School, approaching a bridge over the M25/A21 link motorway, but just before the bridge you come to and turn right onto a track going off to the right, with a gate a short way along it. At last you're back on the course of the old line again; the presence of junction 5 of the M25 makes it impossible to follow the course of the line westwards back to + above with the eyes, let alone the feet! There's no right of way through the gate so please refer to my introductory notes, but once

Storm damaged? A mess of branches and twigs on the approach to Dunton Green from Westerham.

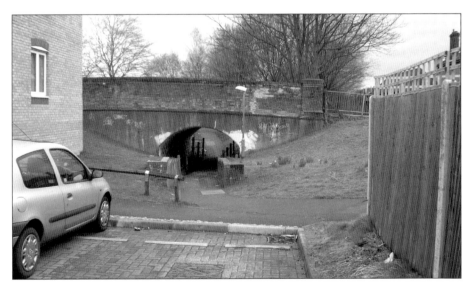

The Westerham-Dunton Green line passing under London Road - a nice example of how old railway engineering has been incorporated into a modern amenity.

you've negotiated it, follow the track just north of east, keeping to the course of the old line. This is lovely easy walking, and it gets better. The track seems to end with an area of thick vegetation ahead, but there is a path into and through the vegetation following the course of the old line on an embankment. In the spring parts of this embankment are carpeted with primroses - a lovely sight which makes the earlier road trudging worthwhile. You have to drop down to cross a stream using concrete blocks as stepping stones, then having scrambled back up the other side you can continue along the embankment - be warned, it could be muddy - going forward into Hillfield Place. Walk along this road to reach what is the only railway paraphernalia left on this line, namely the overbridge carrying Dunton Green's main street over the line. You can make your way under the bridge, just as the trains did, but unfortunately on the other side your way, and the course of the old line, are blocked firstly by a school and its grounds, and then new housing development beyond that; you need to turn right onto the main street, walking downhill as far as the signed road leading to the station. At the station itself, thanks to the new housing, there is no evidence whatsoever of the branch platform. Regular trains run from here to Sevenoaks, from which there are buses available going back to Westerham.

WALK 8 - **TUNBRIDGE WELLS - GROVE JUNCTION**

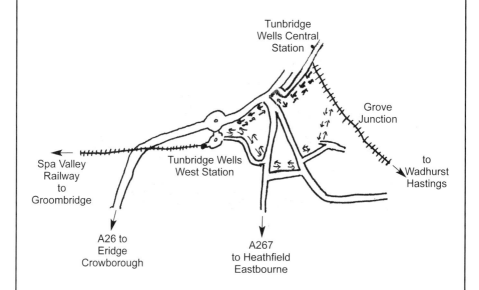

Tunbridge Wells Central Station

Grove Junction

Spa Valley Railway to Groombridge

Tunbridge Wells West Station

to Wadhurst Hastings

A26 to Eridge Crowborough

A267 to Heathfield Eastbourne

Scale: 4·2cm - 1km

WALK 8 - **TUNBRIDGE WELLS - GROVE JUNCTION**

Length:	3.5 miles.
Start and Finish:	Tunbridge Wells Central station.
Public Transport:	Regular trains serving Tunbridge Wells on London Charing Cross-Hastings line.
Refreshments:	Tunbridge Wells (P,C,S).
Conditions:	This is a short and generally easy walk requiring no more than a couple of hours; although much of it is along roads there is a good section of walk along the old line at the end, and there are traces of the old line at many other points. This walk is best undertaken when the Spa Valley Railway (SVR), about which more below, is operational and the engine shed is open, because a tour of the shed and a ride on the train together make a perfect complement to this walk.

History

The disused section of line between Tunbridge Wells West and Tunbridge Wells (actually the last part, into Tunbridge Wells Central, followed what is still operational section of line on the London Charing Cross-Hastings route) was part of a railway that opened in 1866. Back in 1855 the East Grinstead Railway Company had built a line between Three Bridges and East Grinstead, and it was the East Grinstead, Groombridge and Tunbridge Wells Railway Company that built the link between East Grinstead and Tunbridge Wells of which this little section is a part. Groombridge was one of the intermediate stations on this line, and in 1868 the Brighton, Uckfield & Tunbridge Wells Company opened a link line between Groombridge and Uckfield which had been served by rail from Lewes since 1858. Services on the line between Three Bridges and Tunbridge Wells ceased on 1st January 1967 but trains continued to run from Groombridge to Tunbridge Wells via Tunbridge Wells West, starting from Eridge on the London Victoria-Uckfield line. This service ended in 1985, but in due course a railway preservation company was set up and the Spa Valley Railway was born; at the time of writing trains on the SVR ran between Tunbridge Wells West and Groombridge but by the time this book appears services should be available to the Uckfield line at Eridge.

This still leaves a small section of disused line between Tunbridge Wells West and Grove Junction, the junction with the main Charing Cross-Hastings line, and this small section forms the subject matter of this walk.

Walking the Line

Starting from Tunbridge Wells Central station, make for the higher "main road" exit via the steps, turn right to cross the bridge and follow the High Street downhill, swinging sharp right at the end to a junction with the A26 London Road. Turn left, immediately cross the A267 Frant Road exit and continue south-westwards alongside the A26, very shortly reaching a roundabout junction. Turn left here and go forward to reach another roundabout* almost immediately. Straight ahead of you is the former Tunbridge Wells West station building, a magnificent construction which at the time of writing was being developed as a restaurant. Turn left at this second roundabout immediately in front of the station along Linden Park Road, and soon reach a pathway providing the pedestrian entrance to Sainsburys. By detouring right along this pathway and looking right, you can see the patio of the restaurant which marks the platform and course of the old line outside Tunbridge Wells West station, and looking ahead (just south of west) you can see the tracks which have now been incorporated into the SVR, with the engine shed now housing the SVR headquarters and complex just to the right. Return to Linden Park Road and follow it eastwards. You may shortly wish to detour to the right again into a coach park; at the far left-hand end you can see and walk up to the bridge under which the old line went as it continued towards the junction with the still extant

The splendid Tunbridge Wells West station, now looking out rather sadly onto a car park

Hastings-London line. Briefly, therefore, you're able to follow the old line. However there's no way forward under the bridge, so walk back to Linden Park Road and proceed eastwards along it as stated. The road soon forks and you need to swing sharply right into Montacute Road, shortly crossing over the bridge carrying the old line; looking across to the other side, you can see the old line all but lost in thick vegetation. Continue up Montacute Road to the T-junction with Frant Road, bearing right here and then first left into Roedean Road, soon arriving at a T-junction with Warwick Park. Turn left and walk just beyond the right-hand turn (Blatchington Road), to a bridge over the old line; its course going westwards is easy to discern (albeit it's inaccessible) but north-east of the bridge it is another jungle! Retrace your steps very briefly and bear left into Blatchington Road, following it quite steeply downhill to a T-junction with Upper Cumberland Walk.

The sad remains of a bridge crossing just off Blatchington Road on the Tunbridge Wells West-Grove Junction line.

Turn left here to join what in fact almost immediately becomes a pedestrian walkway, and you reach what remains of the bridge carrying the old line over the walkway. On the near(east) side of the bridge and to the right, you can climb a short steep bank and by surmounting or crawling under stout metal railings, you can access the line. However this is emphatically not a designated public right of way, so please refer to my introductory notes. The old line is quite easy to follow, with a crude path through the undergrowth, the going getting easier as the vegetation recedes, and it is actually very pleasant walking. You continue past the backs of houses, the course of the line bending gently left and the going becoming rougher again, but you are in fact able to continue through the trees to the fence beyond which you can clearly see the Hastings line ahead at Grove Junction. This is as far as you can go, and it's now simply a matter of retracing your steps all the way back to the roundabout asterisked above. However, although the walk is at an end, you'll surely want to go forward to the SVR headquarters - just a few yards further on - and enjoy looking round the very impressive range of exhibits including model railway and cinema showing film of the line when it was part of the national network. Then of course you should ride the SVR towards Eridge. Even if you're unlucky and the station complex is shut, you won't have far to go for refreshments, as Sainsburys with its café is just across the huge adjacent car park! Return to Tunbridge Wells Central station the way you came.

WALK 9 - **PADDOCK WOOD - HAWKHURST**

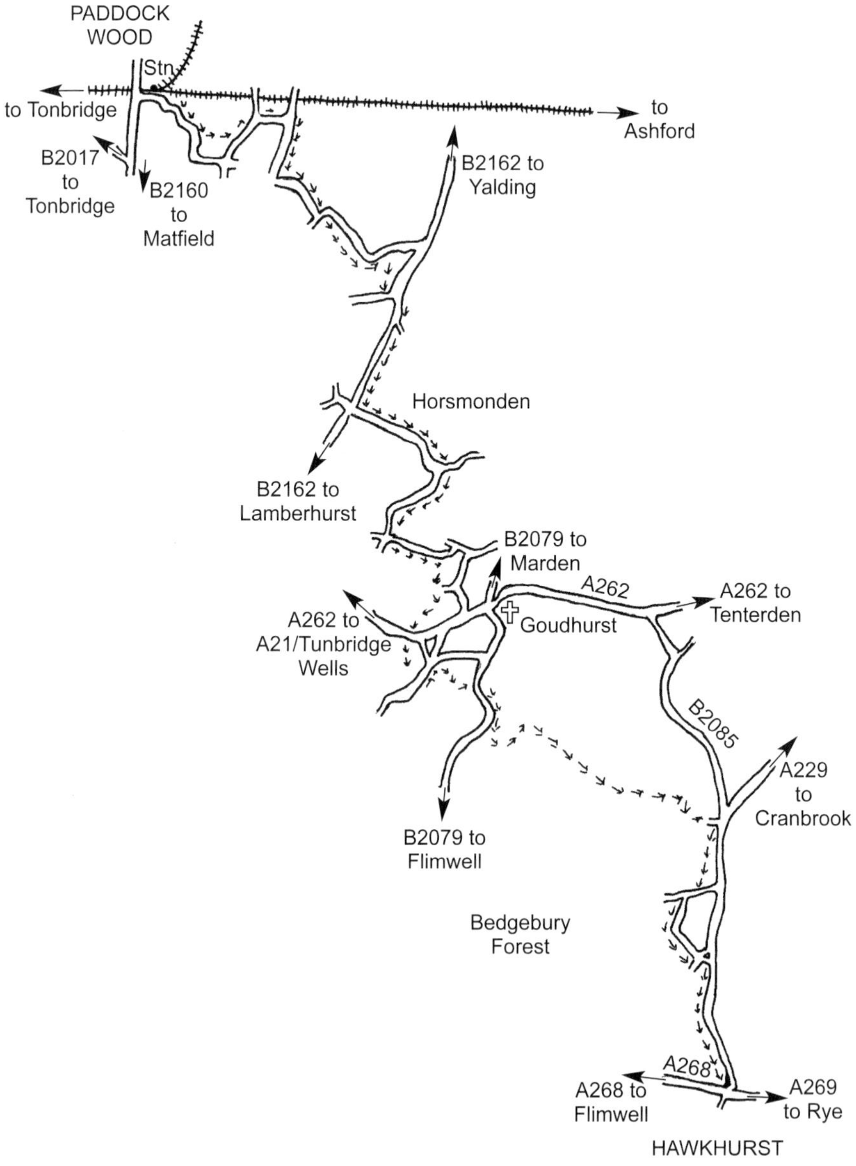

PADDOCK
WOOD

Stn

to Tonbridge

to
Ashford

B2017
to
Tonbridge

B2160
to
Matfield

B2162 to
Yalding

Horsmonden

B2162 to
Lamberhurst

B2079 to
Marden

A262

A262 to
Tenterden

A262 to
A21/Tunbridge
Wells

Goudhurst

B2085

A229
to
Cranbrook

B2079 to
Flimwell

Bedgebury
Forest

A268

A268 to
Flimwell

A269
to Rye

HAWKHURST

Scale: 1·5cm - 1km

WALK 9 - **PADDOCK WOOD - HAWKHURST**

Length:	15 miles (add 2 miles if recommended detours are undertaken).
Start:	Paddock Wood station.
Finish:	Hawkhurst.
Public Transport:	Regular trains serving Paddock Wood and Staplehurst on London-Tonbridge-Ashford route; regular buses(ARR) from Hawkhurst back to Staplehurst on Hawkurst-Maidstone route.
Refreshments:	Paddock Wood (P,S,C); Horsmonden (P,S); Goudhurst Station (P); Hawkhurst (P,S,C).
Conditions:	This walk is manageable in a day but could and perhaps should be split into two days, as there are so many interesting villages and other attractions on or close to the route. It is arguably the most scenic of all the disused railways in Kent, and while there isn't a huge amount of walking on the old line available, there is enough to make it a really rewarding walk, especially in spring, when the blossoms and bluebells are out.

History

Although there had been a lot of talk about establishing a branch line into the Weald of Kent from the main Tonbridge-Ashford line, which had been completed in 1844, it wasn't until 1877 that the Cranbrook and Paddock Wood Company obtained its Act of Incorporation and by 1882 had obtained authorisation to run trains as far as Hawkhurst from Paddock Wood. They chose a hop leaf for the motif of their seal, as if to emphasize what they undoubtedly saw as a significant source of both freight and passenger revenue - the hop industry. Paddock Wood had become a major centre of hop cultivation in the middle of Kent, and hop gardens extended over a large area with Hawkurst within its radius; not only did moving the hops to market require proper transport, but a means was also needed to get hop pickers to the fields, and the line was ideally suited to deal with both these aspects. As a result, thousands of Londoners were able to get out into the hop fields using rail services from the London slums into the Kent countryside, and the hops they picked were able to be collected by rail.

A splendid bridge carrying the Paddock Wood-Hawkhurst line over a farm lane just north-east of Horsmonden.

It was clear that the construction and running of the line could only be achieved with the intervention of one of the "big boys" and indeed the South Eastern Railway duly took the line over. But despite their doing so in the same year as the legal authorisation

Footpath going nowhere - sadly vegetation blocks progress at both ends of this crude path near Horsmonden along the course of the Paddock Wood-Hawkhurst line

was obtained, it wasn't until October 1892 that the line opened as far as Goudhurst, and September 1893 that trains were able to continue on to Hawkhurst. The line's engineer was Colonel H.F. Stephens, well known for his so-called "shoestring empire" of railways, and in the best tradition of Stephens' creations, there was the minimum of earthworks. Two other characteristics of the line were firstly the number of significant inclines, owing to the very hilly nature of the surrounding terrain, and secondly the remoteness of some of the stations from the places they served; the terminus at Hawkhurst was well over a mile north of the village centre, and Cranbrook station was around two miles away from the town of Cranbrook. Initially there were ten trains a day each way, but between the wars the daily service reduced to only six or seven trains each way. In 1922 the timetable showed six daily trains on the line, starting from Tonbridge; the first down train of the day left Paddock Wood at 8.33am and arrived in Hawkhurst at nine exactly. Additionally there were over the years a number of hop pickers' special trains coming down from London. As well as hop-pickers, the two boarding schools in the area, Cranbrook and Benenden, also generated traffic for the line while freight included not only hops but coal, fertilisers, grain and market produce, and near the end of the life of the line, pot-plants were conveyed along the line from local nurseries for Woolworths! The line also found fame in the mid-1950's when Goudhurst station featured in a children's TV drama called The Old Pull And Push. Sadly the 1950's saw a decline in both freight and passenger traffic. Hops had begun to be carried to Paddock Wood by road rather than by rail, and with market produce being carried by road direct to London, coal became the only significant type of freight that

The old station at Horsmonden, the first on the Paddock Wood-Hawkhurst line and considerably nearer the village it served than other stations on this line!

Like a brooding monster, this rather decrepit overbridge towers somewhat menacingly over the Paddock Wood-Hawkhurst line near Finchcocks close to the old Goudhurst station

was carried on the line. During the same decade, numbers of hop-pickers began to fall heavily as living standards rose, and many of those who still came to pick hops had access to their own road transport. The decline in numbers created a vicious circle as farmers resorted to mechanical pickers, so the demand for human pickers naturally went into decline as well and there was no need for "specials" any more. With the increase in car ownership, many people who might otherwise have used the line as a means of getting to Tonbridge or London found it just as easy to drive to a nearby main line intermediate station such as Staplehurst or Etchingham. Quite simply by the end of the 1950's there was no need for the line, which was overstaffed anyway, and the final trains ran on 12 June 1961. Sadly, although some traces of the old line remain, much more has been obliterated, which is a great shame as a footpath or cycle path along the former track would have created a walk of outstanding interest and scenic beauty.

Walking the Line

Make your way out of Paddock Wood station via the main entrance/exit and go forward to reach Church Road immediately, turning left and following it out of the village. Having left the village behind in roughly three quarters of a mile, you pass a little cemetery which is to your left, and just beyond the cemetery turn left onto a signed footpath, keeping a house and then a stream to your right. The path veers right to cross the stream and proceeds just south of east towards farm buildings, with orchards ahead. You reach a T-junction of paths, here turning right and immediately arriving at a road, Queen Street; turn left to follow the road which soon reaches a humpback bridge - your first encounter with the old line. Looking left you can follow the course of the line with your eyes, as it heads across fields to join the main line you have just left. Just beyond the bridge, the road bends left, and as it does so, bear right onto a farm road taking you past the impressive Park Farm. You arrive at a T-junction with another road onto which you turn right and which you follow just west of south; you pass the turning to Great Old Hay and a footpath turning to the left, and soon you get level with the humpback bridge you passed over a little while back. Look to your left and you'll see metalled gates* beyond which the old railway continued. There's no way through, but in fact it is possible to enter the field on your right and walk along the field edges back to the humpback bridge - your first piece of walking along the old line. It is private, so please refer to my introductory notes.

Retrace your steps to the metalled gates asterisked above, turn right and now follow the road a little, but very soon bear left at the next junction to follow Pearsons Green Road, the old line now out of sight for a while to your left. Continue to

Although not a public right of way, this section of the Paddock Wood-Hawkhurst line between Goudhurst and Cranbrook offers some excellent walking.

a signed T-junction, turning left here to enter Churn Lane, which swings right and passes the turning to August Pitts Farm which is to the left. The lane swings sharply left, and as it does so you reach a house called Churn Siding, quite appropriate as the old line crossed the lane here. However, don't pass the house; just before it there's a stile on the right and you cross it to follow a path just south of east (the same direction in which you were following Churn Lane before the sharp bend). You could continue along the path to the B2162 Maidstone Road, and turn right to follow it towards Horsmonden, but it is possible to bear right, just before the path goes behind the grounds

of Orchard House Farm, and follow the course of the old line across fields, aiming for the raised ground to the south where Yew Tree Green Road leaves Maidstone Road. This is private, so refer to my introductory notes, and you need to take care to negotiate a rather awkward ditch crossing. On reaching Yew Tree Green Road, turn left and walk back down to Maidstone Road, turning right. Follow the B2162 south-westwards, passing the Haymans Hill turn to the left, and a couple of hundred yards beyond that turn you reach a lane going off to the right with a church immediately beyond. Turn right down this lane and soon you reach a magnificent brick bridge. You can shin up the bank here and

The Paddock Wood-Hawkhurst line at its loveliest: two beautiful sun-drenched scenes on the approach to Cranbrook station on a spring day.

follow the old line in both directions, although progress back towards Paddock Wood is easier; it is delightful old railway walking with lovely views. Unfortunately whichever way you go, you reach dead ends, so return to the lovely old bridge and retrace your steps to Maidstone Road, turning right to follow it into Horsmonden. Just as you enter the village, you can look to your right to see the old line below you in thick vegetation, but there's no chance of another look at it this side of the village centre. Continue on into the centre of Horsmonden; this is your only on-route opportunity for replenishment of supplies, and the friendly shop can offer you takeaway hot drinks and cakes to enjoy on the seating out the front. Turn left at the village centre into Goudhurst Road and follow it, soon arriving at a yard and industrial unit to the left which is on the site of the old Horsmonden station, with Lamberts Place just opposite to the right. You now lose the old line again, as you proceed south-eastwards along the road, ignoring a turning to the left and dropping down to the Brick Kiln Lane turning to your right, roughly a mile from the centre of Horsmonden. Turn right to follow the lane. Shortly beyond Share Farm, but beyond Nevergood Farm, you'll reach a point where the old line crossed the road, and you can observe its course to the right and the left. It is impossible to join to the right; you could surmount a gate and follow it to the left(please refer to my introductory notes) but after a pleasant stroll through woodland and beside a field, fencing forces you back. Continue southwards along Brick Kiln Lane to a crossroads and here turn left into Smallbridge Road, the countryside here quite delightful, particularly in spring. Follow this road just south of east, crossing the old line again - it is very hard to discern hereabouts - before dropping down to a bridge over the River Teise, crossing the river and continuing until the road swings sharp left. Here, go straight on along a signed path which soon arrives at another road. This is the closest you get to the very pretty hilltop village of Goudhurst, and you could bear left to reach the village, but your old railway route bears right and then shortly right again down the Crowbourne Farm road. Follow the footpath signs carefully to pass round the west side of the farm, then simply continue in obedience to the signposts, back onto the farm road as far as a T-junction and crossing straight over then right over fields, to drop back down to the valley. Bear left on the path along the valley floor to arrive at the A262 road. There's a pub just here and the site of the old Goudhurst station is to your right, the site now occupied by a house called, appropriately enough, Haltwhistle.

Bear right onto the A262 and follow it very briefly westwards then turn left along a signed lane, which is also the turning for Finchcocks; you now have the old railway immediately to the left, although note it is down in the cutting beyond the embankment and can't be followed. However, on reaching a T-junction of lanes, where you need to turn right to cross a stream*, you can see a bridge over the old line just to your left and it is possible to follow briefly alongside the old line south-eastwards, and also drop down a flight of wooden steps to the old trackbed. Disappointingly you reach an impasse so go back to the T-junction and over the stream asterisked above, and immediately then turn left to follow alongside the stream on a delightful marked path. You soon reach Ranters Lane, passing a quite beautiful house to the left; turn left onto the lane, passing

An overbridge on the Paddock Wood-Hawkhurst line just beyond Cranbrook station.

the (here inaccessible) old line, walking past the Risebridge Farmhouse complex and turning first right onto Peasley Lane. When the road bends slightly right, turn right onto a signed footpath which proceeds across the fields just west of south then bears left onto a track, parallel with the old line. As you arrive at a gate** shortly before Bedgebury Road, don't go through the gate but turn right along the field edge to a channel marked as a "Water Hazard;" having crossed over it with care, you could walk back along the old line towards Ranters Lane. It is quite delightful walking in the shade of trees, but again it's not a public right of way (refer to my introductory notes) and you're forced back to the gate double-asterisked above. Go forward to arrive at Bedgebury Road, turn right and follow the road which goes uphill; there's no pavement, and it's a busy road, so this won't be among the highlights of your day.

As you reach the Marlingate Farm complex at the top of the hill, turn left down a lane signed Forge Farm and Furnace Farm. You follow it quite steeply downhill, then as it swings sharply left, you swing with it, to pass the Forge Farm buildings. Just beyond them there's a lane leading off to the right; rather than going straight on you need to take this lane, which proceeds south-eastwards, soon crossing a stream and then rising from the valley floor to meet the top of the cutting above the old line. Looking to your left, you'll see it's quite impenetrable going back towards Risebridge. Keep to the track as it proceeds south-eastwards parallel with the old line, which in any case is down the cutting; a sign warns you to keep out so although there are no physical bars to progress you need to refer to my introductory notes. Now watch carefully, because shortly the cutting diminishes and it's possible to join the old line on a proper track - it's quite clear where this proper track starts, but you just need to keep an eye out for it on the left, and don't get sucked down to the buildings of Furnace Farm. You can now enjoy a superb walk along the old line, the surroundings quite beautiful; this is old railway walking at its best! About a mile from where the track along the old line started, you reach a junction of tracks. You need to bear half-left(not hard left) here rather than go straight over; if you erroneously go straight over you'll soon know you've gone wrong as you reach a dead end. Follow the path which now rises, and passes a very striking terrace of red-brick cottages which are to the right. Immediately beyond the very last, turn right onto an alleyway which then swings right beyond the houses, then left, down to a road. By turning right here you will reach the old Cranbrook station buildings and observe the industrial estate which has built up around the old station. Walk eastwards briefly up the road; it is possible to bear right to access the line near the old station building and follow it south-eastwards to an impressive bridge, but the ground is so rough that further progress is impossible. Return to the old station approach road and follow it eastwards to reach the A229.

The A229 is a horribly busy road but thankfully there's a pavement beside it. Turn right onto the A229 here and follow it briefly southwards, then just beyond the sign for Broom Hill Nursery on the right, turn right onto a signed byway which proceeds very pleasantly south-westwards; initially you go downhill, then uphill, the old line buried in the trees over the fields to the right. You arrive at a road, Park Lane, onto which you briefly turn right, and pass some buildings. Just beyond these buildings to the right there's a little

The old Hawkhurst signal box at the end of the line from Paddock Wood, miraculously preserved despite the line having closed nearly 50 years ago.

opening into some woodland, and you can walk to the top of the cutting and look down at the old line far below you, and the tunnel under Park Lane. It certainly is a lovely spot. Return to Park Lane, turn right and then take the next (unsigned) road left, heading southwards and enjoying good views to the hilltop village of Hawkhurst. The road then swings to the left (south-east) downhill, to pass beneath the old line (inaccessible to all intents and purposes); ignore a turning to the left and arrive shortly at a crossroads, going straight over into Limes Grove and noting the old line hard to your right+ just before the crossing. Follow Limes Grove to the A229, turn right, then turn right again almost immediately to reach the Gills Green industrial estate which was the site of Hawkhurst station. You can see the beautifully preserved old signal box, complete with name plate, in the yard and by walking to the far end of the estate, you can observe how the trains would have come into the station from the point marked + above. Now return to the A229, bear right along it and follow it for a full mile into Hawkhurst which has a good range of amenities and plenty of buses.

WALK 10 - **TENTERDEN - HEADCORN**

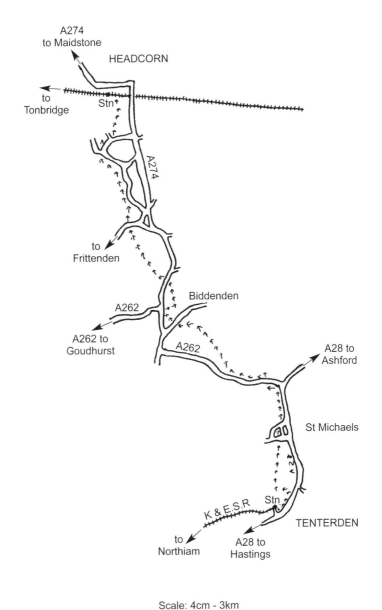

A274
to Maidstone

HEADCORN

to
Tonbridge

Stn

A274

to
Frittenden

A262

Biddenden

A262 to
Goudhurst

A262

A28 to
Ashford

St Michaels

K & E.S.R   Stn

TENTERDEN

to
Northiam

A28 to
Hastings

Scale: 4cm - 3km

WALK 10 - TENTERDEN - HEADCORN

Length:	8 miles.
Start:	Tenterden station.
Finish:	Headcorn station.
Public Transport:	Regular buses (ESCC) serving Tenterden from Rye and on Ashford-Hastings route; regular trains serving Headcorn on London Charing Cross-Tonbridge-Ashford route.
Refreshments:	Tenterden (P,S,C); Biddenden (P,S,C); Headcorn (P,S,C).
Conditions:	This is a walk through classic Kent countryside and contains some splendid sections of walking on the old line itself including a newly-opened section between Tenterden and St Michaels right at the start. With good paths often available when walking the actual line is impossible, there is little need for lengthy road walking. There are some lovely villages on or near the route and it is comfortably achievable in a day.

History

The origins of the Tenterden-Headcorn line go back to 1896 when the Rother Valley Light Railway was incorporated to build a line to link the previously unserved market town of Tenterden with the main network at Robertsbridge. This link was finally achieved in 1903 (its course is almost all in East Sussex and both its history and course are covered in my SB-published book Walking The Disused Railways Of Sussex). In the same year, a Light Railway Order was obtained for an extension to the Tonbridge-Ashford line at Headcorn, and the name of the company was changed to the Kent

An all too rare example of a disused railway in Kent becoming a footpath - a lovely section of path along the Tenterden-Headcorn line on the outskirts of Tenterden

& East Sussex Light Railway. The extension opened on 15th May 1905. There were four intermediate stations between Tenterden and Headcorn, namely St Michaels Halt, High Halden Road, Biddenden and Frittenden Road, the latter two stations well away from the centres of the places they purported to serve! As well as passengers, a variety of freight was carried including sheep from the Biddenden autumn fairs, and domestic coal. For many years the line was managed by Colonel Stephens, who (as is noted elsewhere) managed a number of other railways and who was noted for his zest for economy. It's not surprising, therefore, to note that for a time steam trains were supplemented by model T Ford buses, which evidently were extremely noisy, although these had disappeared by the 1930's. At its peak, there were six daily return journeys on weekdays along the full length of the line, but passenger traffic was never particularly brisk, road alternatives becoming more attractive, and the Tenterden-Headcorn section closed completely in 1954. Although the line from Tenterden to Robertsbridge shut in 1961 the section from Tenterden to Bodiam has since been reopened as a preserved

Two views of the Tenterden-Headcorn line on the approach to Biddenden. Although it's not a public right of way this section is well defined and delightful to walk on

steam railway, a very popular tourist
attraction. There appears to be no
possibility of the Tenterden-Headcorn
section - the subject of this walk -
reopening in this way, but it is gratifying at
least to see that most of the section from
Tenterden to St Michaels is now available
as a public walkway and cycle path - an all
too rare example in Kent!

Walking the Line

The old station at Tenterden at the top end
of the Kent & East Sussex Railway is the
obvious place to start this walk; you can see
the start of the line to Headcorn at the
far(north-eastern) end of the platform.
Walk back up Station Road and turn left to
walk along the attractive main street, going
forward into Ashford Road (A28). Take
what is in fact the first turning left off
Ashford Road, namely Turners Avenue,
and follow it briefly downhill, then as it
swings left turn right into Haffenden Road
and immediately left into Drury Road, a
cul-de-sac. However, just before its end,
swing right and pass through a gate to the
start of a footpath along the course of the
old line. Before joining it, though, it's
worth passing through the next gate and

Where once there were rails, now there are just cart tracks - an easily walked section of the Tenterden-Headcorn line north of Biddenden.

bearing left to follow the left-hand edge of Turners Field to the top, giving a splendid
view of the old station at Tenterden and the course of the line from there. Return to the
footpath and follow it along the old line for about a mile, enjoying lovely walking along
what is an excellent and popular new path. On reaching Grange Road at the top end of
the path, the site of St Michaels Halt, go straight over into Orchard Road and follow it
uphill, then bear right into Shoreham Lane; look briefly left here at what will be your last
glimpse of the old line for a little while.

Follow Shoreham Lane to the A28 and turn left to follow alongside it - thankfully there
is a pavement - then bear left onto the A262 Biddenden Road, with no pavement. It's
a very busy road, so take care. In a few hundred yards you pass High Chimney Farm
which is to the left, and shortly beyond that you reach a sign saying Applegarth Farm
on the right. Follow the approach road into what is a little mini-industrial estate,
actually on the course of the old line, and the site of High Halden Road station.
Continue along the course of the line until a locked gate bars further progress and you

The picturesque wooded approach to Headcorn on the line from Tenterden.

need to bear left along a signed footpath, following a right-hand field edge then walking round the right-hand side of a house to reach the A262 again. Turn right to follow this road for just under half a mile, until you reach Bugglesden Road going off to the left with a signed footpath going off to the right, opposite. Turn right onto this path, initially through a field, then along the left-hand edge of a wood, then north-westwards across fields, passing the course of the old line (access impossible) and forward to follow the edge of a larger patch of wood, north-westwards. Continue as signed, passing through another patch of wood, over a stream, and towards a pond near Washenden Manor. Observing the excellent signposting, veer just north of west through fields, going down to another stream crossing and, aiming to the left of houses, arriving at High Halden Road. Cross over and proceed just north of west along a clear path, going back over the old (hardly discernible) line again and arriving at the pretty village of Biddenden where there are ample refreshment opportunities.

Having enjoyed Biddenden, retrace your steps briefly along the path by which you entered it, but now turn left at the first footpath junction at a stile, just beyond the houses. You strike out north-eastwards, crossing the barely discernible course of the old line again; a pond and enclosure then force you round to the left, and you reach a stile and footpath junction. Here you turn very hard left, not quite doubling back on yourself but heading now in a westerly direction back towards Biddenden, crossing a stile and finding yourself on a section of old line which it is possible to walk very briefly southwards(left) but more meaningfully northwards(right), and very attractive it is. Unfortunately as you reach the main A274 road at the end, a locked gate is in your way; you could surmount it(please refer to my introductory notes) or return to the footpath heading west towards Biddenden and continue to the A274 along that, turning right to follow the A274 to the locked gate. Just opposite here is the site of the old Biddenden station, but there is very little evidence of it left. Continue very briefly along the A274 away from Biddenden but shortly turn left along a marked path which proceeds very pleasantly through the meadow and across the old line again. There is the possibility of following it briefly in each direction but you're beaten back each time, so continue on the footpath beyond the old line to arrive very shortly at a footpath junction, with a signed path heading to the right. You follow this path, shortly reaching the old line again; access to your right is impossible, but by turning left* you can now follow the old line clearly and easily in a north-westerly direction, through most attractive woodland with no difficulty of access and only one very modest fence to surmount. You emerge from the trees and proceed along a field edge, then, keeping the obvious course of the old line beside you, go forward to a road keeping just to the right of the houses by the roadside, accessing the road by means of a gate. No part of the section from the point asterisked above follows designated rights of way, so please refer to my introductory notes.

Cross over the road, observing the site of the old Frittenden Road station immediately opposite. Unfortunately it now becomes impossible to follow the old line for the moment, so join a signed path heading just east of north; you can hug the old line for a while by sticking to the left-hand field edge, but you are then forced to swing round to the right, sticking to the field edge, going forward to a gate. Pass through the gate and then continue (just north of east) to a further gate beside Little Ayleswade where you join a minor road, turning left to follow it past the buildings of Ayleswade Farm and on to a T-junction. Turn left to proceed north-eastwards, crossing the old line once more - there's no chance whatsoever of accessing it - and arriving at a road junction where you turn hard right. Now follow the road north-eastwards to the junction with the approach road to the buildings of Bletchenden, and join this approach road. (If you want a further glimpse of the old line continue eastwards along the road and bear left down the approach road to Park Farm, actually following the course of the old line until locked gates bar further progress. You're forced to retrace your steps to the Bletchenden approach road, and join it.) Follow the approach road until it bends sharply left. Now take the signed path which heads briefly northwards along a track then along grass; veer right, and very shortly left again, then pass through a gate and into a field, aiming for a bridge over the river Beult. The course of the old line is now close beside you to your right, and you'll see that its site as it continues beyond the river is now occupied by a huge industrial building, in fact a dairy. Following the path beyond the river, walk past the dairy which is to your right and swing round to the right, heading briefly for the main road, but a signpost then points you left; Headcorn station is now in view, and you head towards that across the field. You cross a stream by means of a little bridge, and can now observe the continuation of the old line beyond that stream, over to your left. To access it, don't turn left immediately beside the stream but take the next "turning" - in fact just tracks left by the farmer - to arrive at the course of the old line once more. You can backtrack along a good path back towards the dairy again, then proceed confidently north-westwards in the direction of Headcorn station on a clear path through the trees, making a lovely climax to your walk from Tenterden. You can even see what's left of the old platform to your right, although it is in rather a sorry state. Go forward to a flight of steps which takes you over a bridge across a subsidiary line and provides access to up and down platforms at the station. The village, an extremely attractive one with a wide range of amenities, is about 5 minutes walk from the station; follow the approach road northwards from the station and turn left to arrive in the High Street.

WALK 11 - **NEW ROMNEY AND DUNGENESS**

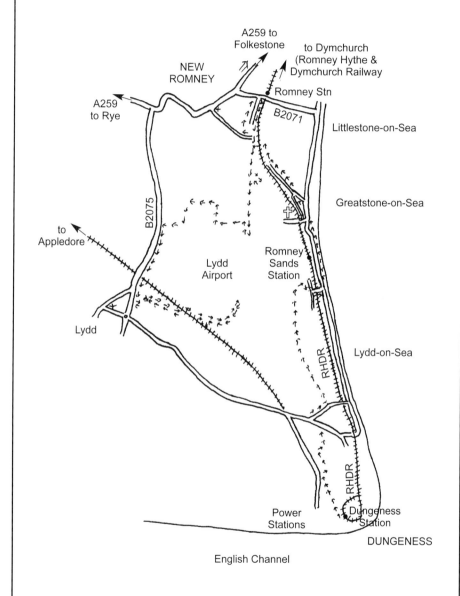

Scale: 2cm - 1km

WALK 11 - NEW ROMNEY AND DUNGENESS

Length:	Minimum 13, maximum 15 miles.
Start:	New Romney station(Romney Hythe & Dymchurch Railway).
Finish:	Romney Sands station(Romney Hythe & Dymchurch Railway).
Public Transport:	Regular buses (SC) serving New Romney and Lydd on Hastings-Folkestone route; regular trains on Romney Hythe & Dymchurch Railway (RHDR) serving New Romney, Romney Sands and Dungeness; regular buses (SC) between New Romney and Lydd via Greatstone-on-Sea. NOTE - in winter the RHDR service is infrequent and often non-existent.
Refreshments:	New Romney (P,S,C); Dungeness (P,C); Lydd (P,S); Greatstone (P,S,C).
Conditions:	What looks on the map to be quite a straightforward walk in easy terrain is in fact surprisingly challenging in a number of respects, with some quite tricky route-finding in the shingle. While large sections of the old lines are available for walking, the interposition of Lydd Airfield presents a major logistical headache. However the proximity of the RHDR and the various attractions at Dungeness more than compensate. It is likely that 2 days will be needed to do it all.

History

Following the opening of the line from Ashford to Hastings in 1851 came the idea of a branch from this line to Lydd and Dungeness, it being hoped that passenger traffic would be generated by the nearby military camp at Lydd and the pilots and fishermen based at Dungeness. The Lydd Railway Company, subsequently taken over by the South Eastern Railway, was floated to construct this line which opened in December 1881, branching off the Ashford-Hastings line at Appledore. There were just two intermediate stations between Appledore and Dungeness, Brookland and then Lydd. Initially, passenger traffic was only conveyed as far as Lydd, and freight all the way to Dungeness, but passenger traffic to Dungeness started in April 1883. A 3-mile branch off this line to New Romney

then opened in June 1884, leaving the Dungeness line a mile beyond Lydd on the Dungeness side. There were no further intermediate stations between the junction and New Romney itself. The Dungeness line and the New Romney branch were in fact served by the same train: sometimes the train from Appledore went either to the one or the other terminus, and sometimes New Romney passengers would get off at Lydd while the train went on to Dungeness, the train then returning to Lydd, picking up passengers for New Romney and making its way there! In 1937 the New Romney branch was realigned, branching off the Dungeness line a further mile and a quarter down the line from Lydd towards Dungeness, and new stations were provided at Lydd-on-Sea and Greatstone on its new

A rare wooded section of the old branch to New Romney from Lydd, just outside New Romney itself.

A more typically open section of the New Romney-Lydd line, along the old alignment, looking south towards Lydd.

A little further down the old alignment of the New Romney-Lydd line. Sadly Lydd Airport prevents a through walk along the old line all the way to the junction with the Appledore-Dungeness line.

branch. At this time Dungeness station was closed to passengers.

The 1920's saw up to nine trains daily between Appledore and New Romney, and on Saturdays it was possible to take a train all the way from Charing Cross to New Romney via Ashford. The 1922 Bradshaw timetable also shows a train, perhaps intended for City gents, leaving New Romney at 8am, arriving in Lydd at 8.07am and going forward to London Cannon Street arriving at 10.04am - while passengers from Dungeness could pick up that train at Lydd using a connecting service leaving Dungeness at 7.47am. Unfortunately the New Romney branch was to be a victim of the Beeching axe, and on 6th March 1967 not only did that branch close but also the section of the Lydd-Dungeness line running from the "new" junction for New Romney to Dungeness. The old and new alignments of the New Romney branch and the now defunct section of Dungeness line from the new alignment junction to Dungeness are accordingly covered by the route description that follows. However, the line from Appledore to this junction remained in use for the conveyance of atomic waste, and still does so today. Happily, Dungeness is now served by rail in a different way, in the form of the immensely popular Romney Hythe & Dymchurch Railway, and coincidentally the RHDR station is immediately adjacent to the site of the former station on the disused line back to Appledore and Lydd.

Walking the Line

It is suggested that the walk be undertaken in two parts. The first part is as follows. From New Romney Station(RHDR), cross straight over Station Road into Mountfield Road and walk down past the industrial estate, which was once the site of the old New Romney and Littlestone Station. Immediately beyond the estate, bear left and then right to follow a crude path through the grass, which goes forward into a strip of woodland through which there's a clear path along the course of the old line with the RHDR to the left. You pass the end of Church Lane and join a track which follows the course of both old and new alignments; however, you will very soon see* a very modest embankment heading away to the left - use as your "marker" the boundary between a cultivated field and rougher grass - and it's possible to follow it, this being the course of the new alignment. In due course it becomes a proper if sometimes rather sandy track, which heads pleasantly towards Baldwin Road in Greatstone-on-Sea, this road dominated by a tall church. In due course a gate and strict "keep out" notices bar further progress, so satisfy yourself with following the new alignment with your eyes aiming just to the right of the end of Baldwin Road. You will return to this area later in your walk. Now retrace your steps back to the point asterisked above, and turn left to enjoy what is now a straightforward walk along the course of the old alignment, fractionally west of south along a clear track. There's just one point where you reach a fence and you're forced to bear right, up to the next track, turning left to go over the ditch and then left again to return to the course of the old line, bearing right to continue along it. Shortly you go over a stream where there's some chunky stone which one guesses was part of an old railway bridge** then continue forward until you reach the Lydd Airfield boundary with no further progress possible.

To pick up the old alignment of the line south of the airfield you now need to get round to Lydd. You could decide to retrace your steps all the way to New Romney and catch a bus into Lydd (ask to be dropped by the old station), but if you'd rather walk, retrace

The course of the old alignment of the New Romney-Lydd line on the south side of Lydd Airport

Wooden posts mark the course of the now dismantled final mile of the Appledore-Dungeness line.

your steps to the point double-asterisked above and turn left. Follow the right-hand field edge, crossing over one track and going forward to a much wider one, turning right and passing a motorcycle racing circuit, then beyond the circuit, take the first track turning left, passing Belgar Farm. Immediately beyond the farm, cross a stream and bear left onto a signed path that heads south-westwards across fields, keeping a golf course to the left, then bears right (westwards) as signed over the field to join the B2075 at Footway Farm. Turn left to follow this rather busy road which passes the airfield and arrives at the old station.

However you've reached the old station, go over the level crossing beside it and forward into Station Road then

A spectacular view of the southern end of the Appledore-Dungeness line from the top of the old Dungeness lighthouse.

immediately left down Harden Road, turning left into Oakham Drive - there is a footpath sign here. You walk down the drive, through a modern housing estate, and pass through a gate at the end. Signing is unclear, but follow the left-hand field edge; at the corner, veer right to continue along the left-hand field edge, until you reach (and undertake) a crossing of the ditch to your left, and beyond that you take the clear path leading across the next field to the next ditch! Turn right to follow the left-hand field edge as far as a bridge that takes you over the ditch, and beyond that the clear path goes forward to run alongside the extant railway. Use the stile to cross it, then follow the path parallel with the railway on the other side, passing through a gate. You are now at the start (or end!) of the old alignment. Do not be tempted to swing away from the lineside at the field edge, but continue beside the old line as though heading for the water tower ahead, then veer left as (not very clearly) signed in a couple of hundred yards, just beyond an area of vegetation to the left. This is in fact the course of the old alignment of the old line, helpfully marked by a row of wooden posts, and it is a very pleasant walk through the shingle, swinging round to head fractionally east of north. Unfortunately fencing prevents your being able to make a link with the northern section of the old alignment, so you're forced to retrace your steps to Lydd. That completes your walk along the old alignment of the line.

Looking north along the new alignment of the branch linking Lydd and New Romney.

The second part of the walk starts at Dungeness station at the end of the RHDR, and it is suggested you make your way there by the RHDR train; although this may restrict the number of days when you can do this walk, a ride on the RHDR is a tremendous experience, very much in keeping with your old railway exploration. You should also go to the top of the lighthouse adjacent to the station, from which, looking north-westwards there is a fantastic view of the terrain through which the old line passed. Make your way to the station car park just to the west of the station exit, and in the broad expanse of shingle and grass beyond the car park, just a little to the west of the RHDR line at the start of its loop route back towards New Romney, you'll see a little raised grassy area with one or two pieces of stone scattered around it. This is in fact the site of the start and finish

A little further up the new aligment of the branch linking Lydd and New Romney with the sprawl of Greatstone-on-Sea over to the right.

of the Appledore-Dungeness branch. Stand on this grassy area, facing in a way that keeps the nearest part of the huge power station complex immediately to your left, and looking on an imaginary line to the northwest, just a little to the right of an imaginary line towards the prominent coastguard cottages, you should see a wide strip of gorse amidst the shingle. Walk north-westwards towards the gorse strip then walk alongside the right-hand edge of the gorse, beyond which, looking north-west, you will see a line of wooden posts which mark the course of the old line. Just before they start there is a very moving and beautiful memorial to a Polish pilot who crashed hereabouts in 1941. Now simply follow the line of posts until you reach fencing*** beyond which the old line continues as part of the power station approach road. At the very last wooden post before the fencing, turn to the right and, taking as your marker a tall brown stone building (noticeably taller than the houses around it), with a small row of upper windows but apparently no windows below, walk down the shingle bank, away from the course of the old line, as if aiming for this tall building.

Keep on in a straight line but as you approach the bushes ahead, look left and you'll see a prominent pump house. Veer left to walk towards the pump house, keeping an attractive lake to your right. Walk round the left side of the pump house and then follow a quite narrow stony lakeside path which very shortly veers right to pass the top end of the lake but with another lake immediately to your left. Having crossed this sort of natural bridge between two lakes, don't turn left immediately but go forward onto a wide band of shingle and rough grass with bushes beyond. As you get to the middle of this band of shingle and grass, allow your gaze to move anti-clockwise (left) and you should see in the distance, separated from you by the shingle/grass band, an off-white building with industrial workings adjacent to it. Head for that building, walking across the shingle - it's actually quite bearable for shingle walking and there is a piece of metal pathway available for part. On the nearside of the off-white building you're aiming for, you should see cars on the unclassified but always busy Lydd-Dungeness road, and you go forward to this road, climbing up a small shingle bank just at the end to reach it. Turn left to follow this road. Continue for a few hundred yards along the road, passing Kerton Road going off to your right and going forward to the large metalled structure on the right marking the place where the extant railway starts and finishes. If you are a purist, you could bear left here down the power station approach road to the point triple-asterisked above, but it has to be one of the most boring pieces of old railway walking in this country! Return to the point where the extant railway starts and finishes, and you can trace the new alignment leaving the "main" line here and proceeding initially parallel with the Lydd-Dungeness Road south-eastwards, ie back towards Dungeness, before heading away from it, parallel with and to the left of Kerton Road which you passed a short while before.

You can now embark properly on the new alignment, aiming just to the left of the works to the left of Kerton Road - signs ensure you don't encroach onto the works! - and keeping them to your right, head just west of north through the shingle beside the fence. It is quite hard going but as long as you keep the fence to your right there is no problem. In due course you're able to access a firmer path immediately to your right which follows the new alignment, past the village of Lade which is to your right, and forward to a big

The top end of the new alignment of the branch linking Lydd and New Romney with the tower of New Romney church in the background.

lake on the left complete with "sounding mirrors" and an explanatory board*+ detailing their origins. Keep going, with the lake still to your left and a profusion of holiday homes to your right; the going gets a bit tougher, with a choice between a "high" and "low" route through shingle, but you are continuing to follow the new alignment all the way to the top of the lake, with good views across the marshes. The OS-marked right of way gives out about a quarter of a mile short of Baldwin Road, and the remaining quarter of a mile or so is over private land, so please refer to my introductory notes. In any event, very frustratingly, with Baldwin Road in view and the course of the new alignment you followed in the early part of this chapter within sight, you find yourself hemmed in by barbed wire and forced back. There are actually no breaks in the fence until you reach a stile just beyond the explanatory board marked *+ above. Cross the stile and aim diagonally half-right(north-eastwards) across the shingle to arrive at the end of one of the roads linking the shingle with Leonard Road, and you duly walk to Leonard Road itself. The top of Leonard Road is a dead end so you need to walk down to Derville Road, turn left onto it and follow it eastwards to the seafront Parade. Turn left onto the Parade and in a few hundred yards, take the first left turning to arrive at Romney Sands station on the RHDR. You can then use the RHDR to return to New Romney station where you started, and enjoy a drink in the café and/or a browse in the excellent station shop.

If the trains aren't running or you are unfortunate enough to have missed the last train, you may be lucky with a bus, but failing that, from Romney Sands station follow the Parade past junctions with Seaview Road and Baldwin Road and bear left into Dunes Road, going forward to a woodland footpath that brings you back to the course of the old and new alignments close to the end of Church Lane. It's an easy walk back to New Romney station via Mountfield Road, or, if you want to go into the centre of New Romney, just follow Church Lane.

WALK 12 - **SANDLING - SANDGATE**

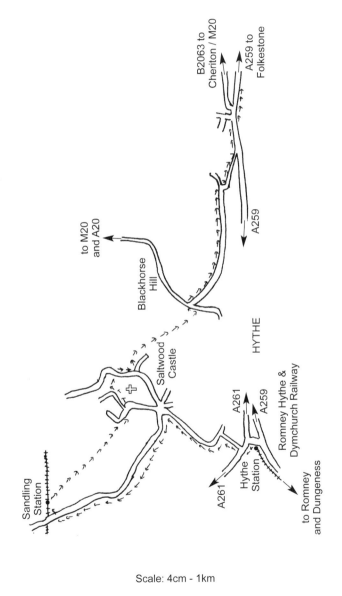

Scale: 4cm - 1km

WALK 12 - **SANDLING - SANDGATE**

Length:	3 miles.
Start:	Hythe station on the Romney Hythe & Dymchurch Railway.
Finish:	Seabrook Road, junction with Battery Point.
Public Transport:	Regular buses (SC) serving Hythe station on Folkestone-New Romney route; seasonal trains on the Romney Hythe & Dymchurch Railway serving Hythe; regular buses (SC) serving Sandgate on Folkestone-Hythe route.
Refreshments:	None on the route itself; plenty in Hythe.
Conditions:	Although not much of the railway is available for walking, this is a splendidly rewarding and easy walk, eminently achievable by most walkers in half a day and possibly less, with lovely scenery, the bonus of an old castle, and lots of pieces of evidence of the old line.

History

Despite being one of the Cinque Ports and a seaside town of considerable importance, Hythe was still not served by rail in the early 1860's, the main line which by then linked Ashford and Folkestone steering well clear of the town. To remedy that omission, and to provide a link with the adjoining settlements of Seabrook and Sandgate, the South Eastern Railway (SER) in 1874 opened a branch line to Sandgate via Hythe (the only intermediate station) and Seabrook, leaving the main line just east of Westenhanger. In fact a station known as Sandling Junction was subsequently built at the junction, and this station, now simply known as Sandling, survives today. There were actually plans to extend the Sandgate branch towards Folkestone but these never materialised. Although by 1922 there were frequent services along the line, with as many as 18 trains each way on Saturdays, passenger numbers were never very high, the problem being the distance between the stations and the places they purported to serve; this prompted the inception of a horse tramway between the centres of Hythe and Sandgate which the SER took over in 1893 but which ceased in 1921. Thereafter, passenger numbers on the railway line did not significantly improve, passengers apparently finding it easier simply to stick to the main line between Sandling and Folkestone and using the intermediate

A rare section of the Sandling-Sandgate line that can be walked, just after the start of the walk from Sandling.

station at Shorncliffe to access Hythe and the adjoining communities. The section of the Sandling line beyond Hythe shut in 1931 and the branch shut altogether for passengers in 1943; although it reopened with a very limited service two years later, it closed permanently for all traffic in December 1951.

Walking the Line

From Hythe station, turn left to follow Scanlons Bridge Road very briefly, then bear left onto the A261 London Road and almost immediately bear right up Barrack Hill, turning left at the T-junction at the end onto Bartholomew Lane, and then at the multiple junction at the top, turn left onto Sandling Road which leads to Sandling station. On reaching the station, turn right through the station car park and go forward onto a marked footpath which follows the course of the old line for a couple of hundred yards. An excellent start! Unfortunately you're forced away from the old line as it disappears into a tunnel; climb the adjacent steps to reach a T-junction of paths where you turn right. Follow the path as it veers downhill, ignoring a path turning to the right, and then proceed along a delightful path which keeps the course of the old line immediately to the left, arriving at a splendid house and here being forced away from the old line again. Bear right to join Rectory Lane, which soon swings left and drops down, with a very pretty church just ahead; walk towards the church then shortly before Rectory Lane swings right, bear hard left onto a signed path which very soon widens into a track and heads north-eastwards. The surroundings here are absolutely beautiful. As the track

The mouth of the tunnel just east of Sandling on the Sandling-Sandgate line.

bends left, look to your left at the course of the old line coming in from the left, then take the signed footpath heading right off the track (effectively, the same north-easterly direction) but then having crossed to the other side of the old line, bear right to follow along the right-hand field edge with the old line immediately beside you to the right. You soon reach Grange Road and turn right to follow it, going back over the old line and, before Grange Road arrives at the right-hand bend, turn left down the Saltwood Castle approach road, keeping the old line to your left.

Fairly soon after joining the approach road, bear slightly left as signed, away from the castle, but keeping it close by you to the right, and now enjoy a lovely walk south-eastwards, with the old line above you and to the left, and attractive meadow scenery to the right. Don't stay on the valley bottom but keep on the hillside, as close to the old railway as possible, and in due course you reach the junction with Blackhorse Hill. Turn left to follow it briefly, then very shortly bear right into Cliff Road (this turning being as near as you get to the site of Hythe station) which you follow for the best part of a mile. The old line ran immediately parallel with Cliff Road to the right, but thanks to modern development, there's absolutely no trace of it now. However the sea views are excellent, emphasizing just how scenic this line would have been. Near its end, Cliff Road swings sharply right - ignore the "No Through Road" track going straight on - and you cross the old line, there being some evidence of it just to your left here, and descend to Seabrook Road, noting on your descent how modern development has again obliterated the old line's course parallel with you to your left. On reaching Seabrook Road turn left and follow it to the next left turn, Horn Street, where you'll see a fine

The view of the magnificent Saltwood Castle which travellers would enjoy aboard the Sandling-Sandgate line.

railway bridge; if you wanted to observe a bit more of the course of the old line you could turn left into Horn Street and immediately left again into Naildown Road then left into Naildown Close, each providing some glimpses of the line. It is all inaccessible though! Return to Seabrook Road and go on to the next left turn, Hospital Hill, which again was crossed by the old line. Finally a little further on down Seabrook Road you reach the junction with Battery Point, the site of the old station, now completely obliterated by modern development. There's a bus stop just a little way beyond Battery Point on the other side of the road, with buses back to the start.

Another fine example of railway engineering on the Sandling-Sandgate line, near the old terminus at Sandgate.

WALK 13 - ELHAM VALLEY LINE AND FOLKESTONE HARBOUR

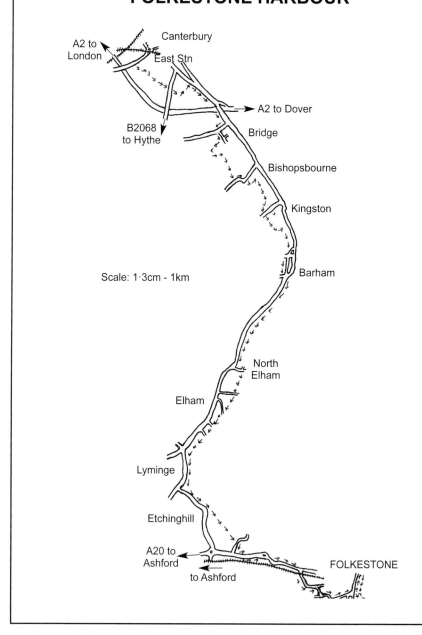

WALK 13 - ELHAM VALLEY LINE AND FOLKESTONE HARBOUR

Length:	17 miles, rising to 21 miles if the suggested detours are undertaken.
Start:	Canterbury East station.
Finish:	Tesco, Cheriton (on outskirts of Folkestone) or Folkestone Harbour.
Public Transport:	Regular trains serving Canterbury East on London-Faversham-Dover line; regular buses (SC) between Canterbury and Folkestone serving Bridge, Kingston, Barham, Elham, Lyminge, Etchinghill and Cheriton; regular trains serving Folkestone Central on London-Ashford-Dover line.
Refreshments:	Canterbury (P,C,S); Bishopsbourne (P); Barham (P,S); Elham (P,S); Lyminge (P,C,S); Etchinghill (P,C,S); Cheriton (P,C,S); Folkestone (P,C,S).
Conditions:	This is a long walk which realistically needs two days to complete. Although there are two good sections of old line walking towards the end of the journey, the amount of walking on the old line itself is very limited. However once you are away from Canterbury the scenery on this route is as good as any on routes described in this book, and public transport links are excellent, giving you considerable flexibility in planning.

History

Although a company had in the 1860's proposed the building of a rail link between Canterbury and the Kent coast in the vicinity of Folkestone, the proposed project had fallen into financial difficulty and was abandoned in 1873. However, in 1881 the Elham Valley Light Railway Company Bill received Royal assent, enabling the Company to proceed with building of a line between Canterbury and Folkestone, and work subsequently commenced. The South Eastern Railway absorbed it in 1884 but owing to difficulties with obstinate landowners it wasn't until July 1887 that the part of the line south of Barham was opened (this joining the main Folkestone-Ashford line just

The delightfully preserved old station at Bishopsbourne on the Elham Valley line.

west of Shorncliffe at Cheriton), and the link with the Canterbury West-Ashford line at Harbledown Junction in the outskirts of Canterbury was achieved in 1889. The last obstacle was a 72ft girder bridge over the river Stour just outside Canterbury. Between Canterbury and the junction with the Ashford-Folkestone line, heading seaward, trains would leave from Canterbury West, branch off the Ashford line and go forward to intermediate stations at Canterbury South (shown in some timetables as South Canterbury), Bridge, Bishopsbourne, Barham, Elham and Lyminge.

The line enjoyed a placid existence and was indeed described by H.P. White as "the epitome of the rural branch line that has now passed away." It came into its own during World War 1 when following a landslip on the main line between Folkestone and Dover, it was used as a means to link these two towns by rail, via Canterbury, Minster and Deal! Things duly returned to normal after the war, the 1922 timetable showing six trains completing the journey each way between Folkestone and Canterbury via the Elham Valley on Mondays to Saturdays. For workers in the city of Canterbury the 7.47am from Folkestone Central, calling at all stations (including Shorncliffe Camp, before the branch off the main Ashford line), reached Canterbury West at 8.37am, and the 5.12pm from Canterbury West would get them home at 5.57pm. During World War 2 the line was closed to passengers as an economy measure; evidently people got out of the habit of using it, for when it was reinstated in 1946 it was very poorly patronised. Passenger services were withdrawn in June 1947 and goods services were withdrawn in October of the same year. Today, over 60 years later, there are still plenty of reminders of the old line in the form of cuttings, bridges and station buildings, with the station buildings at Bishopsbourne and Lyminge still in situ and very well preserved. There is also, uniquely for a disused Kent railway, a museum devoted to it near the southern end of the line. However, as stated above, comparatively little of the old line is available for walking. The main line linking Folkestone with Dover opened in February 1844 and the original Folkestone Harbour station, at the end of effectively a spur off the main line, was opened in 1849. By the start of the 21st century the spur and station had become little used, although the Venice Simplon Orient Express was one of the trains that was seen here. The station and spur finally closed in 2008 although at the time of writing the station buildings and track were still in situ. It could hardly be said to be a discrete branch with a character of its own, but is included in this section simply for interest's sake, making a good optional finale to your Elham Valley pilgrimage. It would be good to think that either in future it could be revived as a railway - the track is still there - or converted into a leisure facility for walkers or cyclists. At the time of writing, however, the future of both spur and station is uncertain.

Walking the Lines

From Canterbury East station, walk down to the roundabout junction with the ring road, Wincheap and Castle Street, and straightaway you have a choice. If you want to do the lot, walk beside the A290 ring road (Rheims Way) heading north-westwards. Cross over the river and, immediately beyond, turn half-left (not hard left) onto a path which goes forward to a hump-backed bridge over the another river. Go straight on beyond that bridge to a children's play area and car park, passing through it to arrive at Whitehall Road beyond. Turn left to follow the road, soon passing under the Faversham-Canterbury East line, keeping the Ashford-Canterbury West line to your right. You see

A beautiful and walkable section of the Elham Valley line between Kingston and Barham

a level crossing gate sign ahead but well before the crossing there's a gate and stile to your left. Go over the stile, turning half-left to aim for and scramble onto an embankment carrying the first section of the Folkestone branch off the Ashford-Canterbury West line, albeit you can't see the actual join. It's a very pretty embankment walk above the Stour meadows but there's no way over the Stour and the upshot is you have to walk all the way back to the roundabout just below Canterbury East station, the same way.

Now, whether you decided to make the initial detour or not, head south-westwards down Wincheap (A28), and turn right into the retail park down Ten Perch Road, the last turning before the A2 bridge. At the very bottom you arrive at Staples superstore; walk on down in the same direction to the right of the store and you'll arrive at the meadows on the south side of the river. By turning right you can see the old railway embankment on the other side and how it continued on your side, petering out in the retail park. Return to the road through the retail park but turn left now into The Boundary; as Cotton Road leaves it to the left, you could detour up the last (dead end) part of The Boundary parallel with the old embankment which is to your left. Retrace your steps and turn right into Cotton Road then next right into Cow Lane (you can detour briefly right into Maiden Lane for a further look at the old line to the right, but you need to go back to Cow Lane) and follow Cow Lane to return to Wincheap. Cross over into Hollow Lane but immediately bear left onto an alleyway which roughly follows the course of the old line (the old line itself becoming quite untraceable in the housing estate, veering off to the right) and arrives at the bottom of Valley Road. Walk along

One of the loveliest spots on the Elham Valley line just south of Barham; the fence on the valley bottom marks the course of the old line.

The approach to Elham on the Elham Valley line.

Valley Road, turning first right into Elham Road and following it to its end. Turn left at the end up an alleyway, Hop Garden Way, then bear right at the end into Heaton Road; follow it to its end, going forward along a footpath to a T-junction with Lime Kiln Road. Turn right then almost immediately right at the path fork, soon emerging into a rough green open area. Pass between the metal poles to your left, dropping down into a little dip then rising again, bearing left and heading south-eastwards on a clear path along the left-hand edge of the open area, the old line parallel with you to your left. You arrive at Stuppington Lane; note the brick bridge to your left, and see how the old line cutting has been "filled in" over time.

Now you must lose the old line as its course has been covered over by the Kent & Canterbury Hospital (the former Canterbury South station sited immediately north-westwards of and adjacent to the hospital complex), so turn right into Stuppington Lane and follow it downhill. It veers left and then sharp right, and at this sharp right-hand bend you turn left onto a lane; follow this lane, which soon veers right and then left, and comes to a large barrier with FOOTPATH ONLY inscribed on it. Pass it and almost immediately arrive at a T-junction with a metalled alleyway. Turn right onto it and follow it south-eastwards keeping the buildings of Simon Langton Boys' School to your right. You reach the west end of Langton Lane and turn left onto it, soon arriving at a T-junction with the B2068 Nackington Road and going straight over onto a lane which strikes out south-eastwards. It peters out at a T-junction with a green field-edge path; turn left and follow the path north-eastwards, passing over the course of the old line (itself inaccessible here). You go forward to arrive at a roundabout junction and turn right here to follow the A2050 New Dover Road, the old line parallel with you to your

For just a little while The Elham Valley Way follows the Elham Valley line - here is part of that section of the Elham Valley Way near Lyminge.

right. Fortunately a pavement is available. As you approach the bridge over the A2, look out for and turn right onto a lane signed for Renville; follow this lane briefly westwards then turn sharp left to cross the A2 and approach some buildings*. By bearing right along the track to the right of the buildings, you can return to and briefly join the old line by descending steeply down the bank. However it is a steep drop and you're unable to follow the old line north-westwards or for more than 100 yards or so south-eastwards, so return to the buildings asterisked above. It should be possible for you to turn right and walk past the farm buildings then bear left to reach the top of Bridge High Street, turning right to follow it towards Bridge. Otherwise return to the A2050 and turn right to follow it, crossing over the A2 and then bearing first right to access the top of Bridge High Street.

Now follow Bridge High Street towards Bridge, but before reaching the village you need to bear right at the first crossroads onto Station Road, then bear first left onto Pett Hill and follow it until you reach Union Road coming in from the left. Immediately opposite, turn right onto a path which soon crosses the course of the old line. (The old station at Bridge was just a little further up the line to the right as you cross it.) Just beyond, turn hard left onto a path which proceeds very attractively south-eastwards, parallel with the course of the old line, and arrives at a T-junction with another path. Bear left and cross back over the old line** but immediately having done so you can quite easily drop down to access the old line and follow it for a little under a quarter of a mile north-westwards (back roughly in the direction you've come) or for a slightly longer distance south-eastwards. However, you should note that there is no public right of way along the old line here, so please refer to my introductory notes. Sadly you're unable to proceed further either way (vegetation to the north-west, a tunnel mouth to the south-east) so retrace your steps and follow the path eastwards from the point double-asterisked above. At the next path junction, immediately beyond the hop plantation, turn right onto an excellent clear path with the plantation to your right and Bourne House and its park to your left. You arrive at the buildings of Lenhall Farm; you bear right into the complex, then left to follow the farm approach road south-eastwards, the old line now to your left having emerged from the tunnel.

When you reach the T-junction at the end of the farm approach road turn left onto Crows Camp Road which shortly bends sharply left, and there's a wonderful surprise: as you cross the old line, you can look down to your left at the superbly preserved Bishopsbourne Station. Sadly it is private so you will have to make do with observing it "from above!" Continue over the bridge and immediately bear right onto a signed path across a field, then bear left through a gate onto a lane which drops downhill, going forward to the metalled Park Lane and arriving at The Street at Bishopsbourne. There's a pretty pub on the corner. Turn right onto The Street then, as it bends left, go straight on along the signed Elham Valley Way - you'll see a lot more of this route as you continue. Follow the Way south-eastwards though the lovely Charlton Park, then, emerging from the park, you reach the edge of a very large field with the Elham Valley Way straight on and a public footpath signed half-right across the field. Don't take either of these routes but bear hard right along the right-hand field edge to arrive at the course of the old line and then turn left to follow the old line as far as a sign indicating the proximity of the village of Kingston. Go right here onto a path that goes down steps then across a field to reach Kingston's village street; turn left along the street then, with the church in sight ahead, bear right onto a signed path. Don't follow it down towards the church but rather remain on the right-hand field edge and then turn right onto the obvious well-defined railway embankment. It's now possible to enjoy a delightful walk on a well-maintained path along the course of the old line, passing over Covet Lane and going forward along a good clear track, continuing to follow the course of the old line. Sadly you're forced to bear left, down to Valley Road; turn right to follow it to Barham, the (inaccessible) old line parallel with you to the right.

You continue alongside Valley Road into Barham. When you reach the village centre, look out carefully for and follow The Causeway, a narrow road to your right just beyond Heathfield Way (also to your right). Almost immediately you reach a crossroads; by detouring right here you'll join the appropriately-named Railway Hill and can observe the railway crossing of this road with the site of the old Barham Station immediately to your right. Whether or not you made this detour, you now head south-westwards from the crossroads along South Barham Road, the course of the old line immediately parallel with you to your right but imperceptible in the fields. From the T-junction at the end of South Barham Road, however, it is possible to discern its course past the South Barham Farm buildings immediately to your right, but it's not feasible either to join the line or follow it further from here. Instead, bear left at the T-junction and then hard right onto the main road which runs through the Elham valley and which you now need to follow for about 2 miles. The old line runs parallel with it to the right, and close by all the while - usually in the field immediately adjoining the road - and on occasion you can see the course it would have followed, in the form of overbridges and adjacent tracks. However, none of the old line is designated as a right of way: there are a number of obstructions, and it is a good deal easier just to stick to the road from which you can observe the line and its surroundings. Although it's a minor road, it is a busy one, so take care. You pass a vineyard (where refreshments may be available); a little further on is the former Palm Tree pub, and not far beyond the former pub is the hamlet of Wingmore where there's a road junction which you cross straight over, keeping to the same road.

Shortly beyond Wingmore the old line crossed from the right to the left of the road - the line of trees in the field to the right being the obvious indicator - and a little beyond that there's a lane going off to your right leading to Worldswonder Farm. The road then rises, and you reach a footpath sign with metal signplates pointing up a path to the north-west and one to the south-east (which is the path you want). Watch carefully out for, and cross, the stile in the hedge to the left just past the footpath sign, and walk south-eastwards through the field downhill to reach the valley floor again. Bear right to very briefly join the course of the old line, bear shortly left then veer right to pass a large new house which as you'll see has been built on the old line, and go forward to arrive at the little village of North Elham. Turn left onto the road, then shortly before the next road turning to the left, bear right as signposted onto the Elham Valley Way. This curls round the backs of the houses on a right-hand field edge to rejoin the course of the old line, and follows it on a good clear path to reach Duck Street at the east end of Elham, where the old station was sited. Although to continue to Folkestone you need to cross to the south side of Duck Street, it's likely you'll want to stop off or even call it a day here; to access the very pretty village of Elham, simply turn right up Duck Street and ascend to the village centre.

On the other (south) side of Duck Street, your path on towards Folkestone is a narrow green strip first between houses and then to the right of a narrow stream, contrary to what is shown on recent Ordnance Survey maps (which shows the path running to the left of the stream). The old line is initially to your left but crosses the path, quite imperceptibly, before you reach the next road junction. Now back on the Elham Valley Way, which took a slightly different route through Elham, cross more or less straight over the road and proceed very pleasantly south-westwards; the course of the old line is down to your right on the valley floor, alongside the Nail Bourne stream. Still on the Elham Valley Way, you cross another road, then go forward to cross one further road, now finally able to access the old line again, the Elham Valley Way following it quite delightfully across fields to Lyminge. As you arrive at Lyminge, the old line veers slightly away to your left, but you go forward to join a metalled lane and follow it to the bustling

This name plate at Lyminge, by the Elham Valley line, says it all!

main street of Lyminge. Having reached the main street, turn left to follow it. You'll be unable to rejoin the old line for a good mile or so, but don't miss the opportunity to detour up Station Road to see the old station building (now the village library), the car park behind which is built on the old line. Return to the main street and follow it south-westwards out of the village, soon reaching the houses at Broad Street; immediately past the houses, turn left onto a signed path which leads across a golf course towards the golf clubhouse. Notice how the character of the landscape has now completely changed. Keeping the (inaccessible) old line to your left, veer to the right of the clubhouse and through the golf club car park to reach Canterbury Road at the north end of the village of Etchinghill. Turn left to follow the road uphill along the pretty village street and away from it, heading south-eastwards. As the road rises beyond the village and approaches a sharp right-hand bend, look out for a path going off to the left carrying the Elham Valley Way, North Downs Way AND Saxon Shore Way! Walk down this path which soon reaches the gates of Coombe Farm. Turn left here over a stile but do not follow the signed paths steeply downwards; having enjoyed the splendid view which on a clear day will extend to the sea, follow the left-hand field edge more or less on the same course as the pylon lines, to a locked gate and fence. Climb over the gate and you'll find yourself back on the old line. Since there is no public right of way over this gate, ideally permission should be sought - please refer to my introductory notes - but it is well worth it. The old line is followable for only a few yards going back (left) towards Etchinghill, but is easily followable south-eastwards (right) towards your ultimate objective and you can enjoy some of the best disused Kent railway walking there is, along a lovely clear path with good views through the trees to the rolling hills. Continue to follow it (in due course being joined by the Elham Valley Way) to the road junction at its very end where there's a nice surprise in the form of the Elham Valley Railway Museum on the left. Sadly it is only open at weekends, April to August, but a visit here is an ideal complement to your walk and a good excuse for a rest.

Unfortunately you must now lose the old line, since immediately to the south-east of this point it has been swallowed up by the extensive workings of the Kent terminal of the Channel Tunnel. With regret, therefore, turn right onto Newington Road and follow it through the pretty village of Newington to reach the very busy A20. Turn left to walk briefly alongside the A20 using the pedestrian footway and passing under a bridge carrying access roads to the terminal and also the Channel Tunnel railway line; as you emerge from under the bridge, follow the Elham Valley Way signs to bear right, cross the road with great care and go straight on along a footpath over the M20 motorway. Once over the motorway, you immediately arrive at a footpath junction. Turn left here to follow a path parallel with the motorway. The path arrives at a road coming in from the right; cross over the road and continue alongside it in the same eastward direction, passing a Holiday Inn and then the Saga building known as Cheriton Parc House. Immediately beyond Cheriton Parc House bear right into the car park and then very shortly left, following signs for "Visitors Bays 13-18." Aim for a red/orange CCTV sign ahead and follow the path which continues on into a pleasant park area, and by continuing through the park alongside the fence to the left you are actually on the course of the Elham Valley line for the last time, as it meets the main Ashford-Folkestone line coming in from the right. Please note however that although there are no obstructions to access this is not a public right of way and you should refer to my introductory notes. Retrace your steps to the road and then bear right along it, shortly arriving at a Tesco superstore in the suburb of Folkestone known as Cheriton.

At Tesco you have a choice. By proceeding eastwards along Cheriton High Street you'll soon reach a bus stop providing direct buses back to Elham and Canterbury; this bus route passes through most of the villages you'll have enjoyed on your walk, enabling you to relive your old railway exploration. Alternatively, as you're in the area you can take the opportunity to proceed down to Folkestone Harbour either by bus from Tesco or on foot to view a piece of very recently disused spur linking the main Folkestone-Dover line with Folkestone Harbour. (If accessing the harbour on foot, continue beyond Cheriton High Street into Cheriton Road then just beyond Folkestone West station on the right, bear right into Beachborough Road, and follow this road to the roundabout junction with Castle Hill Avenue. Turn right into Castle Hill Avenue and follow it over a double roundabout to reach the Leas; turn left here and descend to the harbour.) Make your way to the landward end of the harbour wall and enter the harbour area, bearing right to access the (at the time of writing) derelict and very sorry-looking Folkestone Harbour station. Follow the platform seawards then at the barriers turn right up stone steps to reach the harbour wall, and follow it out towards the lighthouse, keeping the course of the old line beyond the station down to your left. You come to a dead end so retrace your steps, exit the harbour area and turn right into Harbour Approach Road, the old line on a separate, very impressive bridge over the water to your right. Indeed it is worth visiting the spur just to view this bridge. Go forward from Harbour Approach Road up firstly Harbour Street then The Tram Road to your right, with the old line immediately beside you on your right. You pass under Radnor Bridge Road and continue up The Tram Road to the point where the road bends sharply left; it's impossible to follow the old line any further inland other than with your eyes, so retrace your steps, bearing hard right into Harbour Street and forward into Tontine Street to access the centre of Folkestone. ALTHOUGH IT IS TECHNICALLY ACCESSIBLE AT SOME POINTS, DO NOT ATTEMPT TO WALK ALONG THE LINE ITSELF. At the time of writing, pedestrian access to it is still forbidden although future use of the line is uncertain and it would be good to think that if the railway is not revived, the spur or at any rate part of it might become a pedestrian walkway or cycle path.

A splendid brick underbridge on the Elham Valley line between Etchinghill and Newington.

WALK 14 - **CANTERBURY - WHITSTABLE**

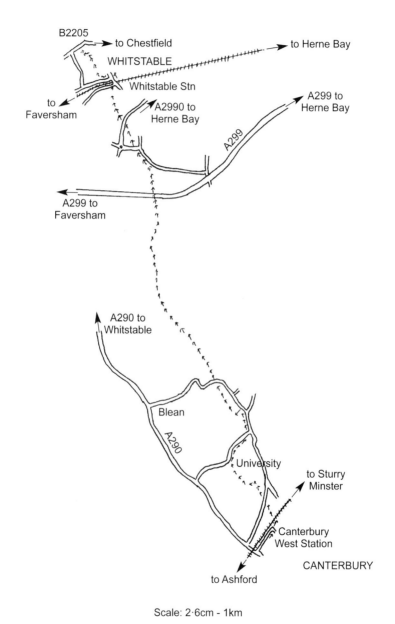

Scale: 2·6cm - 1km

WALK 14 - CANTERBURY - WHITSTABLE

Length:	8 miles.
Start:	Canterbury West station.
Finish:	Tower Parade, Whitstable.
Public Transport:	Regular trains serving Canterbury on London-Ashford-Ramsgate and London-Faversham-Dover lines; regular buses (SC) back to Canterbury from Whitstable; regular trains serving Whitstable on London-Faversham-Margate line.
Refreshments:	Canterbury (P,C,S); Whitstable (P,C,S).
Conditions:	This is one of the best disused railway walks in Kent. The course of most of the old line is easily traceable, and there is some excellent walking available on the old line itself. There are also very good public transport links, the surroundings are delightful and there are many reminders of the old line throughout. You should be able to complete the walk in half a day, but it's worth setting a day aside in order to enjoy some time in Whitstable, one of the most charming towns on the Kent coast.

History

The line linking Canterbury and Whitstable is one of the oldest railway lines in the world, and was the first public steam-powered passenger and freight line in the south of England. As early as 1823 Canterbury's city council was being urged to consider a rail link to the coast, silting being a constant problem for shipping between the nearby town of Fordwich, which served as a port for the city, and the open sea. In June 1825 the Act incorporating the Canterbury & Whitstable Railway Company received Royal assent and work began on the line, only for the work to be suspended in 1827 through lack of funds. However in due course the work was completed and in May 1830, to the echo of celebratory Cathedral bells and guns fired in salute, the line opened and passenger services commenced. In due course the railway company was absorbed, and services taken over, by the South Eastern Railway. Initially the line was worked by a combination of cable and stationary engines, with locomotives taking over in April 1846; Robert Stephenson's "Invicta" was one famous visitor to the line in its early years. Originally the Canterbury terminus was in North Lane, a little to the south-east of the extant Canterbury West station, but when the South Eastern Railway between London and Ramsgate arrived, also in 1846, the terminus was diverted so that trains branched off the new London-Ramsgate line using a short bay at the end of the down platform at the new Canterbury West station. Between Canterbury and the first station, Blean & Tyler Hill Halt, there was a tunnel (known as the Tyler Hill tunnel) nearly half a mile long; this would of course have been a novelty for passengers, and it was certainly not universally popular. There were further halts at South Street in the outskirts of Whitstable, and Tankerton, just beyond the point where the Faversham-Margate line (when completed) passed underneath the Canterbury-Whitstable line. The terminus at Whitstable, known as Whitstable Harbour, was situated quite close to the waterfront just to the east of the town centre, and a harbour was built in connection with the railway, being used for the import of coal, timber and grain. In due course a new passenger terminus south of Tower Parade was built, with tracks crossing the road to reach the harbour.

Passenger services on the "Crab and Winkle" line, as it was nicknamed in recognition of the popularity of this seafood with visitors to Whitstable, were uncomfortable and slow, the journey of just over 6 miles taking 20 minutes. However, they were not infrequent, with 9 return trips on weekdays in 1922, increasing to ten on Saturdays with five on Sundays. Inevitably the line faced competition from faster and cleaner buses after World War 1 and services were withdrawn for passengers in January 1931, although freight services - comprising predominantly grain being conveyed to a mill in Canterbury - continued until December 1952. Ironically it was temporarily reinstated the following year to bring coal to Whitstable while the main line through the town was closed due to flooding. Then in 1974 subsidence of the Tyler Hill tunnel caused damage to college buildings which had been constructed over the top of it; the old line was not going down without a fight! Fortunately, the trackbed did not become obliterated by development as so many disused sections of old railway in Kent have done, and it is now recognisable for much of its length. Better still, sections of it have been incorporated into a cycle track known as the Crab and Winkle route, after the affectionate name given to the line.

Walking the Line

Turn left out of the forecourt of Canterbury West station and follow Station Road West to the mini-roundabout. If you want to proceed direct towards Whitstable, skip to the point asterisked below. If you wish to see the site of the original terminus of the old line, bear right and walk down to the next mini-roundabout, bearing right again into North Lane. Follow North Lane until shortly on the right you reach a gate which, appropriately enough, looks a little like a level crossing gate. This marks, very approximately, the southern terminus of the old line. Turn right to pass to the side of the gate and go forward to a road which you follow as it swings round to the right, then take the first left turn

Beautiful mixed woodland on the Canterbury-Whitstable line.

to return to Station Road West. Now turn right again to follow this road to the mini-roundabout, new development to the right covering the course the old line previously took until the main Canterbury West-Ramsgate line was built. *Now, whether you've detoured to North Lane or not, go straight over the mini-roundabout into the Spires and very shortly bear left onto the signed cycle route. You pass underneath the extant Canterbury West-Ramsgate line, just east of the point where the re-routed Whitstable line branched off it, and continue along the cycle path, soon reaching a large green recreation area. Turn left to follow the left-hand (southern) edge of the green until you come to an embankment that's thick with vegetation. This is the first section of old line still visible; it is in fact possible to scramble up the embankment and walk along the top of it, keeping a cycle track to your left and the green to your right. As the embankment nears its end on the approach to Beaconsfield Road, you need to bear left to scramble down onto the cycle path. Follow it to Beaconsfield Road and turn left to follow the road very briefly, then bear right onto St Michael's Road; just past house number 20 on the right-hand side, bear right onto an alleyway which gives you access to the old railway embankment again. Turn left to follow it. It's lovely walking in the shade of trees - a taste of further joys on this walk - but unfortunately when the embankment path reaches a junction with a lane, within sight of a school just ahead, you have to leave it (the course of the old line going forward to shortly enter the so-called Tyler Hill tunnel).

Bear left along the lane until you reach a crossroads junction with the signed cycle route, and here turn right along a clearly-defined cycle path which proceeds uphill to enter the University of Kent campus. Your path passes the Mandela building which is to your left, reaches a roundabout and goes forward to Giles Lane which has the feeling of a campus drive rather than an ordinary public road. Turn right along it, following signs for Herne Bay, with university buildings on both sides including the Gulbenkian Centre on your right. You reach a T-junction with Canterbury Hill and turn left to follow it downhill, soon reaching a fork junction, and here turning left. Follow this road, Calais Hill, very briefly, then take the first footpath leading off to the left; this is absolutely charming, running parallel with a babbling stream and then climbing a flight of steps to arrive at the old line once more. By detouring left along it you will shortly reach the mouth of the Tyler Hill tunnel, but to make progress turn right (north-westwards) and follow what is a good and well-defined path in the shade of trees, along the course of the old line. Note that this path is permissive, owned by the University, and a sign says the right of access can be revoked at any time. At the top end of this path you reach Tyler Hill Road and cross it, going more or less straight over up a driveway for "The Halt;" there was indeed a halt here when the old line was running. Although it looks private, there is no difficulty with access up the driveway.

How you continue further now depends on the state of the fields. The optimum route crosses a stile to the left of the driveway, just before the gates leading to the house, and bears immediately right to cross another stile and enter cornfields. Now simply follow the right-hand field edge or the cart tracks. The course of the old line is very clear to your right, in the form firstly of a green track (not accessible) and then a modest and heavily wooded embankment. You descend gently to cross a ditch then proceed through a lovely tunnel of woodland to reach a crossroads of footpaths* from which you progress by continuing straight on. *Note, however, that there is no public right of way from Tyler Hill Road to the point asterisked (please refer to my introductory notes); moreover, progress may be difficult or impossible if corn or other crops are being cultivated. If you are unable or unwilling to take this route from Tyler Hill Road to the point asterisked, there is an alternative as follows. Cross the right-hand rather than left-hand stile at the top of the driveway leading to The Halt and follow a clear footpath to arrive shortly at Fleets Lane. Turn left to follow this very pretty lane, the course of the old line marked by a line of trees to the left across the fields. In a few hundred yards you arrive at the buildings of Well Court. Don't go up to the house but bear hard left with the lane and just before the greenhouses turn hard left again along a narrow but well-defined grassy path. This proceeds through a field to arrive at the course of the old line at the point asterisked above, and here you turn right.*

Now proceed in a north-westerly direction along the right-hand field edge, keeping the course of the old line to your right, in the trees. It is not really practicable to follow it as there is too much vegetation. Also note, however, that there is no public right of access to the field edge (again, refer to my introductory notes). Shortly beyond a track which goes off to the left, you reach what looks like an impasse, with a sign (facing the other way) confirming that there is no right of access; however by bearing right at this sign, you will be able to identify and join the course of the old line and proceed to enjoy one of the best sections of disused railway walking in Kent. Simply now continue north-westwards, soon being joined by the signed cycle track again (which you lost at the University) and veering northwards. You are surrounded by beautiful mixed woodland, you have a clear path, and your only concern will be to avoid being knocked over by cyclists, as many cycle enthusiasts use this route. All too soon your lovely path leaves the course of the old line but you actually need to stay on the signed (and obvious) cycle path, looking out for the yellow "Crab and Winkle" symbols on the signposts and not being tempted onto other paths leading off to the right and left. Assuming all is well, you will arrive at and cross a bridge over the A299 north Kent coast bypass, but by looking to the left here you will observe the course of the old line, not only in the form of a strip of thick vegetation but, in the cornfields beyond on both the south and north sides of the A299, an elongated hump through the field marking the old embankment.

Your excellent cycle path - you will wish all your railway walking could be like this! - goes forward beyond the A299 crossing to reach South Street. Turn left to follow South Street to its junction with Millstrood Road which goes off to the left (there was a halt at this junction). Don't continue along either road but go straight on into Invicta Way, a comparatively recently opened footpath/cycle route, which once again sees you on the course of the old line. It isn't as scenic as earlier but it is lovely, easy, safe walking, your path proceeding under the A2990 and continuing on into Whitstable. In due course the cycle path veers away left, off the course of the old line, to join All Saints Close, but you as a walker can continue along the embankment path, dropping down at the last moment to the road known as Bridge Approach. Directly ahead of you is the extant Faversham-Margate railway.

You might think that this was the end of the so-called Crab and Winkle line and that it simply joined the main line here, but in fact it did not; it went over the main line and continued seawards, and there is still a little more of it to see. To access it, turn right onto Bridge Approach, turn left at its end to cross the extant railway, then turn very shortly left into Teynham Road, using the right-hand pavement. Soon the road dips and you will see the impressive remains of a bridge carrying the Crab and Winkle line over this road. Tankerton Halt was adjacent to this bridge crossing. Immediately before the bridge remains, turn right onto a pathway; it doesn't look hugely promising, but there appear to be no bars to access and you can now walk side by side with the old line as it proceeds towards the sea. You can imagine the excitement which must have welled up among the passengers as the train proceeded along here, getting ever closer to the water. Again it's not really practicable to follow the old line itself because of the vegetation, and sadly there's a bit of an anticlimax at the end, when the embankment fades away with no further traces of the old line to be seen, thanks to new development. However there is one consolation: going forward into a new housing estate you'll notice it's actually marked CRAB AND WINKLE and bearing left at the end (as you have to do) you'll see a sign for The Sidings. Now turn right into Station Road and follow it

A good part of the Canterbury-Whitstable line has become a cycle track and an immensely valuable leisure facility. If only the same could be said of other disused railway lines in Kent!

seawards, the last few yards of the course of the old line alongside to the right. Bear left into Westgate Terrace but almost immediately bear right past the Health Centre to reach Tower Parade; the re-sited terminus adjoined Tower Parade just to the right here on the south side of the road. To access the delights of Whitstable and its excellent bus service back to Canterbury, just head westwards along Tower Parade and go forward into Harbour Street and the High Street.

Walking disused railways in Kent can be frustrating. This clear unobstructed path near High Halden (walk 10) soon fizzles into a dead end, and it will be some miles before the old line becomes walkable again.

Some significant stretches of former passenger railway line in Kent have become freight only. This one such stretch, at Lydd, shortly before the point where the now defunct Romney branch (walk 11) leaves it.

WALK 15 - **MARTIN MILL - DOVER**

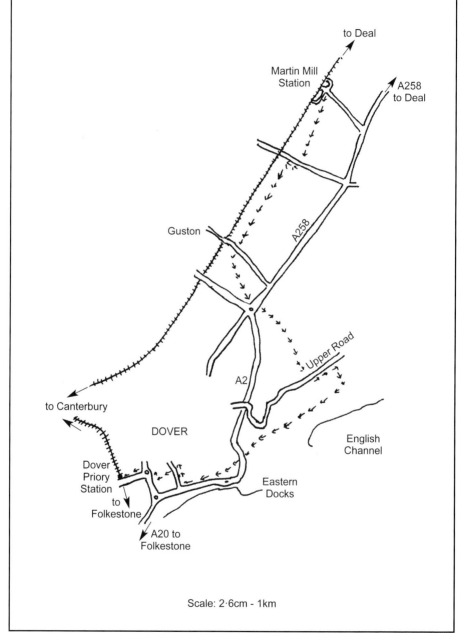

to Deal

Martin Mill Station

A258 to Deal

Guston

A258

Upper Road

A2

to Canterbury

DOVER

English Channel

Dover Priory Station

to Folkestone

Eastern Docks

A20 to Folkestone

Scale: 2·6cm - 1km

WALK 15 - MARTIN MILL - DOVER

Length:	Minimum 5 miles, maximum 6 miles.
Start:	Martin Mill station.
Finish:	Dover Priory station.
Public Transport:	Regular trains to Dover Priory from London, Canterbury, Ashford and Folkestone; regular trains to Martin Mill on Dover Priory-Ramsgate line.
Refreshments:	None en route but plenty in Dover itself.
Conditions:	A very enjoyable and rewarding walk, with a surprising amount of up and down work. It is worth setting aside a full day for the expedition, for although the walk itself should not take more than half a day, you should allow time to explore Dover, one of the most fascinating towns in Kent.

History

In 1897, work began on the so-called Admiralty Harbour, an eastern extension of the harbour at Dover. The contractors S. Pearson & Son needed to bring in gravel to make the concrete blocks for the breakwaters, and in order to transport it from a pit near the town of Sandwich, on the Dover-Ramsgate line, they built a branch from Martin Mill, also on that line. This effectively provided a reasonably direct link between the main line and the site of the new harbour. The first part of the new line was conventional enough, but in order to descend to the docks it needed to zigzag down the sheer cliffs. Although the line closed in 1909 when the harbour works were completed, a company called the Dover, St Margaret's and Martin Mill Light Railway were that same year granted powers to operate passenger trains under a Light Railway Order. However, despite extensions of time being granted right up to November 1946, no passenger service was ever established. Part of the route did reopen during the First World War for use by the military, but the track was taken up in 1937; ironically part of it was relaid in the Second World War, again for military purposes, chiefly to enable the Royal Engineers to deploy rail-mounted artillery. For a line which has seen no use at all for over 60 years, there is a surprising amount of evidence of it that's still visible, making this a very rewarding walk.

Walking the Line

Exit Martin Mill station and go straight down to the (at the time of writing) sadly defunct Ugly Duckling pub. Bear a little to the right of it and walk just west of south down Old Roman Road, going forward to join a well-defined footpath which rises to reach Pond Lane. As you approach the road, look to your right and you'll see a caravan park; the course of the old line left the extant Dover-Ramsgate line just south-west of Martin Mill station and went through what is now the caravan park. (Although the caravan park can be accessed, it is impossible to follow the course of the old line through the park, and the route described above is greatly to be preferred.) Turn right into Pond Lane and go downhill to very shortly reach the remains of the bridge carrying the old line; immediately before the bridge remains, turn left onto a signed footpath which now follows south-westwards beside the course of the old line (marked by the hedgerow) pretty much all the way to the next road, The Lane.This is really lovely walking in attractive countryside with good views down to the course of the extant Dover-Ramsgate line and beyond. Initially, you should keep to the left side of the hedgerow along a right-hand field edge, but then when the path on this side peters out, shift to the right side of the hedgerow along the left-hand field edge. In due course you approach a dead end, with a fence blocking further progress, so transfer your allegiance back to the right-hand field edge on the left side of the hedgerow! The path becomes better defined now, veering slightly left, away from the course of the old line, to reach The Lane.

At The Lane, turn right and walk briefly down to the remains of the old line's crossing

Two underbridges, one still there, carrying the extant line between Dover and Deal, and the remains of another which carried the long defunct Martin Mill-Dover line.

of this road; immediately beyond the remains, turn hard left up a track, now keeping the course of the old line, in the form of a strip of trees, hard to your left. Very shortly another strip of trees branches away to the right. Do not be lured away beside this strip, but turn left up a well-defined path and then very shortly bear right so you are walking to the left of the first strip of woodland along a right-hand field edge heading south-eastwards. Looking across to your left, you should obtain a clear view of the disused and sail-less Guston Mill, while if you look to your right, into the strip of woodland, you'll see the railway cutting, providing clear evidence of the course of the old line. You could of course choose to drop down the cutting and walk along the course of the old track bed, but it isn't to be recommended because of the profusion of vegetation and lack of views; much nicer to view it from above and enjoy the Kent countryside around you! In any case the strip of woodland comes to an end, so simply continue along the right-hand field edge to arrive at the busy A258. Note that although at the time of writing there was no fencing to negotiate to reach the A258, it is still a bit of a scramble through the undergrowth between field and road, so watch your feet. Cross the A258 with great care and turn right, very briefly following this road until you come to a signed footpath going off to the left. The railway actually passed under the A258 just here and you can see the bridge remains poking up through the undergrowth. Turn left here* to follow the signed path, still following the course of the old line. The signed path shortly goes away to the left** but you do not veer left with it(see below). The course of the old line veered a little to the left (eastwards) here then veered in a more south-easterly direction, keeping to the hilltop, and the more direct route described below runs more or less parallel with its course.

Your next objective is now Upper Road, effectively the coast road between Dover and St Margaret's at Cliffe, but although you'll be able to look ahead and see cars on this road in the distance, getting there may be a problem. Signage at the time of writing suggests that this area is used by the Ministry of Defence. However when I walked this section (August 2009) the obstacles, such as there were, were quite easily surmountable and there was no sign of MoD activity. To reach Upper Road by the direct route across this land, continue past the point where the signed path veers left (double-asterisked above) and keep walking along the left-hand field edge. Maintaining the same direction(and parallel with but a couple of hundred yards from the course of the old line), three obstacles have then to be negotiated in close succession: you need firstly to climb over a gate, then go forward to pass a gap in a barbed wire fence, and finally go over a stile to arrive at a metalled drive, with three very imposing masts immediately to your right. Turn left onto the drive, then very shortly reach a junction of metal driveways, turning right to proceed towards the road. Cross a cattle grid by a gate to reach a T-junction of tracks, turning left to arrive at a gate beside two memorials, and cross over the gate to arrive on Upper Road. It must be emphasized that the wisest and safest course is to seek permission before following the route described in this paragraph and if you're in any doubt, it is best for you to use the italicised route below. In any event, you should refer to my introductory notes.

If for any reason the walk from the double-asterisked point above proves impracticable or impossible, return to the single-asterisked point above, and turn left to follow the A258 to a roundabout junction with the A2. (There is a service station here where refreshments can be obtained, so there is some consolation to being forced to go this way!) Go straight over the roundabout and continue along the A258 for barely quarter of a mile until you reach the main entrance to the Duke of York's Royal Military School on your right. Immediately opposite is a track going off to the left; follow this track downhill, parallel with the A258 initially until you reach some farm buildings, and here you continue along the track as it veers left through the farm buildings and downhill towards a tunnel under the A2. Just before the tunnel bear right onto a signed path along the left-hand field edge, parallel with the A2, and follow it for just under a quarter of a mile. At the bottom corner of the field, look carefully for the path going forward through the bushes up a flight of steps to reach Upper Road just west of a bridge over the A2. Turn left and continue along Upper Road over the A2, swinging southwards and shortly swinging sharply northwards (past the entrance to the popular White Cliffs Visitor Centre) then north-eastwards, past the three masts alluded to above and on to be reunited with the direct route at the roadside memorials. This detour will add a good extra mile to your walk.

Follow Upper Road briefly north-eastwards from the memorials, looking out carefully for the next gate in the fence on the left, just a couple of hundred yards beyond the memorials. This marks the approximate spot where the old line met Upper Road. Immediately opposite the gate turn right onto a narrow metalled path which strikes out towards the cliffs and the sea. In a hundred yards or so, look carefully for a clear path going off downhill to the right, the narrow metalled path off Upper Road bending slightly left at this point; turn right here, and now head resolutely south-westwards, getting your first views towards Dover and its spectacular cliffs and docks. Although traces of the old line have long gone, the path you are now taking follows pretty closely the course it would have taken as it zig-zagged down the steep hillside. Straight ahead of you and up on the highest clifftop is another big mast. Do not be tempted onto the path leading up to it, but continue downhill, hugging the bottom of the face of the almost sheer Langdon Cliffs on which the mast is built, keeping the cliff face immediately to your right. The old line continued to the left (downhill) of your path and a little beyond the mast, but there is no trace of it now whatsoever. You can only marvel at the engineering feat which made it possible! You should also enjoy the magnificent views to the Eastern Docks, a constant hive of activity with cars and lorries heading towards, or away from, the cross-Channel ferries.

Now you just need to get to Dover. The suggestion is that at the next path junction, with a choice of a green path straight downhill or a chalky path forking half-right you take the latter, going uphill a little, keeping the cliff-face hard to your right, and arriving in an area of quite thick vegetation. Having risen you then drop down sharply to a metalled footpath punctuated with steps, and turn left to follow this footpath, now going resolutely downhill, under the A2 and forward to reach Athol Terrace. Go straight on

- don't bear left to the roundabout - along East Cliff, a pleasant street of sturdy brickbuilt houses, at last arriving at the A20, the main coast road through Dover. Don't cross the road but bear right alongside it, soon reaching the A256 Woolcomber Street; turn right onto this street, then second left into Castle Street which takes you into Dover's main shopping area. At the big square turn right up Cannon Street then at the crossroads bear left into Worthington Street, very soon arriving at a roundabout. Go straight over onto the B2011 Folkestone Road, and shortly you'll see Dover Priory Station signed off this road to the right. As stated, however, Dover is such a fascinating place that you will surely want to explore some of its history before heading home.

A clear footpath along the course of the Martin Mill-Dover line on the approach to Guston.

WALK 16 - EAST KENT COLLIERY LINES

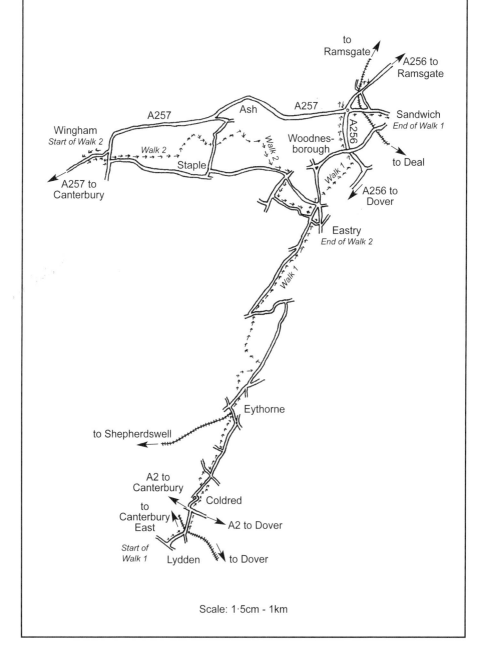

Scale: 1·5cm - 1km

WALK 16 - **EAST KENT COLLIERY LINES**

**Length of description 1
(see below):** 10.5 miles (add 2 miles for suggested detours at the end of the walk).

**Length of description 2
(see below):** 5.5 miles.

**Start of
description 1:** Lydden.

**Finish of
description 1:** Sandwich.

**Start of
description 2:** Wingham.

**Finish of
description 2:** Eastry.

Public Transport: Regular buses (SC) serving Lydden on Canterbury-Dover route; regular trains serving Sandwich on Dover-Ramsgate line; regular buses (SC) serving Wingham on Canterbury-Sandwich route; regular buses (SC) serving Eastry on Deal-Sandwich-Ramsgate route.

Refreshments: Eastry (P,C,S); Sandwich (P,C,S); Wingham (P,S); Ash (P,S).

Conditions: Although there's a very strong link between the two lines described in this chapter, they are both long walks and it isn't really practicable to walk both in one day. The walk from Lydden to Sandwich will require up to a full day if you are to incorporate a ride on the preserved railway from Eythorne to Shepherdswell and back, as well as an exploration of Sandwich. The walk from Wingham to Eastry can comfortably be walked in half a day. There aren't many traces of the old lines and there's a lot of road walking involved; however there are several interesting features on or close to your walk, and the countryside is often extremely attractive.

A pleasant wooded section on the East Kent colliery line between Eythorne and Knowlton.

History

The lines described in this chapter all owe their origins to the discovery of a coalfield in East Kent in the 1890's. Two firms anxious to exploit the coalfield obtained Light Railway Orders to permit rail access to coal supplies in areas not already served by rail; these Orders provided for a line from Shepherdswell (on the existing Canterbury-Dover railway) to Wingham Colliery, via Eastry, and a separate line going off from Eastry to Richborough. The lines were constructed extremely economically with very basic stations and the minimum of earthworks. The reason for the choice of Richborough as one of the termini was to enable coal to be exported from Richborough Port, on the Kent coast between Sandwich and Ramsgate. Between Shepherdswell and Wingham Colliery there were stations or halts at Eythorne, Elvington, Tilmanstone Colliery, Knowlton, Eastry South, Eastry, Woodnesborough, Ash and Staple. In 1920 authorisation was obtained to continue this line to link with the existing Canterbury-Ramsgate line, but in fact only a section to Wingham village itself (the terminus there known as Canterbury Road, with an intermediate stop at Wingham Town) was completed. The line going on from Eastry to Richborough had intermediate halts at Poison Cross, Roman Road(Woodnesborough) and Sandwich Road.

The line from Shepherdswell to Wingham Colliery opened in November 1912 for goods and October 1916 for passengers, with the extension to Canterbury Road opening in 1925. The 1922 Bradshaw timetable shows just two through passenger trains a day between Shepherdswell and Wingham Colliery, at the start and end of each day, reflecting the fact that most passengers would have been workmen. The line from Eastry to Richborough opened for goods in 1916, and to passengers in 1925, but only as far as Sandwich Road. Besides the "main" lines to Richborough and Wingham, there were further branches to local collieries which were authorised by later orders, including Guilford just south of Eythorne, Tilmanstone just north of Eythorne, and Hamil near Eastry(there being no trace whatsoever of the course of this latter branch, so it is not referred to in the description below). These branches did not have a passenger service as such.

Coal provided by far the most common type of freight on the trains, for obvious reasons, but considerable quantities of general freight were also carried. Most of the passengers were miners en route for the collieries, and in the late 1920's workmen outnumbered "ordinary" third-class passengers by nearly six to one. Numbers of "ordinary" passengers dwindled still further during the 1930's and services became even less frequent. Guilford Colliery was largely unproductive and had become derelict by 1937 with trains correspondingly having ceased to run along this freight-only section. The section between Eastry and Sandwich Road, which had only opened for passengers in 1925, closed for passengers at the end of October 1928, but freight continued to be carried from Eastry to Richborough until October 1949 and from Tilmanstone to Eastry until July 1951. Passenger services from Shepherdswell to Canterbury Road via Eastry continued until the end of October 1948, while freight services from Eastry to Canterbury Road closed in July 1950. Finally, the freight link from Shepherdswell to Tilmanstone just beyond Eythorne closed in 1984 during the miners' strike of that year and never reopened. However, the section of line from Shepherdswell to Eythorne has been reopened as a preserved line, and it's hoped to extend it to Tilmanstone in future. It seems convenient to split the descriptions into two, description 1 covering the disused sections between Eythorne and Richborough via Eastry including the Guilford Colliery branch, and description 2 covering the section between Wingham and Eastry from which walkers could of course continue on to Sandwich using the relevant part of description 1.

Walking the Line 1

Your walk starts by following a section of the old branch linking Guilford Colliery with Eythorne, a surprising amount of evidence of which remains. From the Bell Inn at Lydden, bear left (north-eastwards) up Church Lane, passing the church, crossing the railway and climbing steeply Coldred Hill to the A2. Cross straight over the road with great care, then bear left and immediately right along Church Road to enter Coldred; the road bends and passes a pub, and very shortly beyond the pub you bear right along a very clearly marked footpath. It crosses fields and enters a patch of wood, and almost immediately you'll see a gully below you marking the course of the old line linking Guilford Colliery with Eythorne. It is not reasonably practicable to follow the course of the line eastwards to Guilford Colliery from here, as it has been completely lost amongst cultivated fields to the right, but to follow its approximate course with your eyes, continue through the little area of woodland and immediately on emerging look to your right over the fields. The colliery was not much more than half a mile away to the right. Continue along the footpath as marked, keeping houses to the left and shortly crossing two stiles as directed by arrow signs, going forward to arrive back at Church Road. Bear left and follow Church Road briefly south-westwards as far as the bungalow "Hours" on the left-hand side. Immediately opposite "Hours" on the other side of the road is a strip of vegetation between two fields. Go to the right of that strip of vegetation and follow to the right of it, along a left-hand field edge; the strip of vegetation to your left is the course of the old Guilford Colliery branch which soon becomes a proper embankment and is possible to follow in parts as it swings from north-west to north-east. As you proceed, you will cross the course of the North Downs Way national trail.

You arrive at a road onto which you turn right, and go up to the crossroads by Coldred church. Bear left and walk north-eastwards along Coldred Road, the old line parallel with you to your left in the field, then in just under half a mile bear left - the first left turning - onto a road through woods. Follow the road briefly until you come to gates on either side of the road in a couple of hundred yards, pass round or through the right-hand gate, and beyond it follow a track which is the course of the old line. When the wood relents, keep along the right-hand side of a strip of vegetation which marks the course of the old line; continue along the left-hand field edge until you hit a clearly-defined footpath coming in from the left just below you. Turn hard left onto this footpath, effectively taking a hairpin bend, and follow it into a wooded area for no more than 60/70 yards or so. Then, shortly before the woodland relents to the right, turn hard right onto a fairly clear path through woods on what is once more the course of the old line. You emerge into a field but there's a clearly-defined path heading north-eastwards across it which you follow, aiming for and entering another strip of woodland and going forward (still on the course of the old line) to reach a lane. By detouring left you'll almost immediately see the extant line between Shepherdswell and Eythorne and the join between it and the Guilford Colliery branch you've been following, but you need to turn right here onto the lane. As soon as it emerges from the trees in just a few yards, turn half-left over an insulated electric fence stile and follow it across the field aiming for a further stile and gate. Cross the stile, go through the gate and bear left along a clear track to the road. Bear left and immediately you'll see Eythorne station on the left, and the continuation of the old line towards Tilmanstone and Eastry to your right, the track soon to be submerged by vegetation. If you're lucky or have planned your visit carefully, you could now break off from your walk for a trip to Shepherdswell on the preserved section of old line from Shepherdswell to Eythorne; even if the trains aren't running you'll probably want to inspect the old station.

Whether you ride the train or just look at the station, return to the road and turn left to follow it down to a crossroads in the centre of Eythorne. At the time of writing the village pub, at the crossroads, had shut, giving the centre of the village a rather melancholy feel. Turn right at the crossroads into Wigmore Lane and follow it north-

The line of trees to the left marks the course of the East Kent colliery line between Knowlton and Eastry.

eastwards (the course of the old line to your right but inaccessible) until you reach Elmton Lane going off to your left. (By detouring a little further you will see the remains of the bridge crossing of the old branch which served Tilmanstone Colliery; this branch now disappears into an industrial estate and there are no further followable traces of it.) Don't follow Elmton Lane, but just before it walk up onto the old railway embankment which runs just to the left (west) of it, and you are now able to follow the old line through the trees on what is a good embankment path. You're now on the original "proper" line linking Shepherdswell and Wingham Colliery. When the embankment path peters out, veer just to your right to walk parallel with the embankment, beside a high metal fence to your right beyond which is the Tilmanstone Industrial Estate, the site of the old colliery.

The path turns sharp right, away from the course of the old line, progress beside which is really impracticable because of the spoil heaps blocking the way. While the heaps can be negotiated at certain times, they are potentially dangerous, especially in wet weather, and I do not recommend your attempting them. Therefore head eastwards with the clear path back to the road; turn left to follow it and then turn left again down the next (signed) lane. This heads downhill, past Beeches Farm which is to the right, then starts to rise, and as it emerges from the trees you cross the course of the old line, marked only by the line of trees heading off to your right. It appears possible to follow the old line to the next road junction, but to do so would require negotiating fields which may be thick with growing crops, and there is fencing beyond them which was just about negotiable

A good open section of the East Kent colliery line between Knowlton and Eastry; the Richborough power station can just be seen in the background.

at the time of writing but which may well have been reinforced in future. Therefore, I do not recommend your attempting to take this course. Instead, continue north-westwards on the public right of way, heading steeply uphill, giving you a chance to look back at the course of the old line as it travelled eastwards through the fields; go to the crest of the hill, passing under the pylons, then drop slightly to reach a byway and turn right to follow it. Although you can't see the old line, this is a lovely path which drops gently down to arrive at a road junction, the old line coming in to join you from the right. Immediately before the road junction was the site of Knowlton Halt.

Cross straight over to follow Thornton Lane (signed Eastry 2¼ miles). This is a really enjoyable road walk, as it is a very narrow and extraordinarily quiet road, the old line parallel and very close to you on your left. You reach a footpath signed to the left in just over half a mile; you could turn left to follow it, then right to follow beside the old line as it veers a little from but still roughly parallel with the road, its course reasonably clear and marked, to begin with at least, by a line of trees. However, although this is scenically very attractive with lovely views ahead, it may be impossible if crops are being grown in the fields, in which case you'll have to stick to the road. In any event you'll be forced back to the road by the profusion of undergrowth. Continue along the road down to the outskirts of the large village of Eastry; you pass to the west of it, through the Gore district of the village, keeping to the same road and ignoring turnings left and right. The old line is clearly marked to your left through the fields by a line of pylons which follows its course exactly. As you proceed through Gore, just over a quarter of a mile after the start of the built-up area, look to your left for a road signed "Selson $^1/_4$;" you could turn left here, bear shortly right into a field++, and use the field to access the embankment of the old line along which there's a clear, excellent path. There was a halt here, and this is also the point at which the lines divided, with the line to Wingham going off to the north-west - see below. Unfortunately, to exit the path and return to the road, you will have to bear left and then immediately right along the edge of private property and through private gates. PERMISSION IS ESSENTIAL. If you get it, pass through the gates and turn right onto the road to arrive at a crossroads;* if you don't, you'll need to backtrack to the Selson road, follow it back to the road through Gore and then bear left to follow it to the crossroads asterisked above. The old line went over the crossroads, and there was a further halt here (Poison Cross).

From here, proceed northwards along Foxborough Hill, signposted to Woodnesborough; the old line is now to your right and superbly marked by the line of pylons heading south-west to north-east. In barely a quarter of a mile, opposite Hill Cross Farm, turn right along a signed and extremely clear path - a toll route for horse riders. This proceeds confidently and simply north-eastwards to arrive at a T-junction of paths just before the very busy A256 Sandwich bypass; turn left at this path junction and follow a good clear field-edge path, keeping the A256 immediately to your right all the while. The old line, having left the pylons behind, veered northwards along a course roughly parallel with and immediately to the right (other side) of the A256, keeping a straight course to what is now a roundabout junction of the A256 and A257.

A rare piece of (with permission!) walkable East Kent colliery line at Eastry, taken from very close to the site of the junction where separate lines went off to Wingham and Richborough.

It is impossible to follow it meaningfully so stick with your excellent path beside and to the left of the A256, passing a road crossing (the site of another halt serving Roman Road, Woodnesborough) and a path crossing, going all the way to the roundabout junction with the A257. This roundabout is on the site of Sandwich Road Halt, which was the end of the line for passengers.

The old line, as stated above, did continue to Richborough Port for freight only. In theory you could continue northwards along the old line by following a lane just to the left of the A256 as it sets off from the roundabout towards Ramsgate. However the lane is heavily gated and comes to a dead end anyway when you reach Goshall Stream with no way across (the line crossed the stream then turned eastwards below Richborough Castle, its site clearly visible ahead, and then veered north-eastwards to Richborough Port), so you'll have to backtrack. Sadly there really is no more of the old line that can fruitfully be explored. Therefore, whether or not you've made the detour to Goshall Stream, head eastwards from the roundabout along The Causeway, pass over the level crossing with the extant Sandwich-Ramsgate railway line, and simply continue along the road into Sandwich with its attractive streets, good range of facilities and public transport links.

Walking the Line 2

From Wingham church walk down the A257 out of the village towards Canterbury, passing a garden centre which is to your left; the old line passed through what is now the garden centre to end/begin on the north side of the A257 by a footpath sign shortly before a right turn to Ickham. This was the site of Canterbury Road station, the end of the branch from Eastry. Retrace your steps to the sharp left bend of the A257, going forward to join a footpath (ignore one heading southwards just before). Your path soon veers right, then left to reach a school, then right again, passing to the left of the school, then left through a cemetery, the course of the old line just to your right here but not possible to discern. Go forward to the B2046, cross it, turn left then take the first right turn into Staple Road and follow it; the embankment of the old line is clearly visible to your right but not accessible. As the road bends sharp right at Dambridge Farm, continue forward eastwards along a very wide track. The old line (as extended to Canterbury Road) comes in from your right and soon, quite imperceptibly, crosses the track*, veering away to your left and dropping gently to the valley to eventually keep a parallel course with yours. Wingham Colliery Halt was situated close to the asterisked point while the colliery itself, for which there was a spur, stood between your track and Staple Road to the right just here. The colliery itself has now been redeveloped, and neither the line extension nor the spur into the colliery itself are realistically accessible or followable here. In just over a mile from Dambridge you reach the isolated house at Groves, but just before it the wide track veers left with a narrower track continuing eastwards. You stay on the wide track which now heads downhill to cross firstly the course of the old line of which no trace exists hereabouts, then the Little Stour. Climb gently, keeping

A lovely walkable section of the old East Kent colliery line between Staple and Ash, with Ash church forming an impressive backcloth.

to the track which veers to the right of the buildings of Great Pedding Farm to reach the farm approach road. Turn right and almost immediately reach a T-junction; turn right again and walk down to the hop machine, turning left immediately before it onto a clear path with hops to your left and orchards to your right. Turn right at the end then shortly left along a clear path to reach the road at Durlock. The halt at Staple was immediately to the west of this road, a little further down the road where the old line crossed it.

Cross straight over onto another clear path that soon reaches the Poultons Farm approach road, the old line (sadly still inaccessible) coming in to join you from the right. You now go forward along a path through a delightful green recreation area, with the buildings and prominent church of Ash just to your left. For the first time you're actually on the old line. Sadly that doesn't last as the old line becomes inaccessible to the left then veers away imperceptibly to your right; you cross a driveway (with a strict notice warning against trespassers) then bear immediately right onto a path which goes parallel with the driveway. You cross the course of the old line, the old Ash station sited just here, and go forward into a field, the southward course of the path very clear, the course of the old line now to your left. You soon cross a ditch then immediately beyond the ditch turn left onto a farm track which heads south-eastwards. You cross the Little Stour and keep it to the right, shortly arriving at a gate; a notice on the gate says NO ENTRY so you should seek permission to continue (and also refer to my introductory notes). Go through or round the gate to proceed south-eastwards on the track, now following the course of the old line which has rejoined you from the left, and perhaps pausing to look back and enjoy the lovely view of Ash church. On reaching the road turn left (the old line now veering away to the right). Turn right at the next crossroads to join another road, soon crossing the course of the old line (Woodnesborough station sited just to the right of the road here), then take the first left road turning, signed EASTRY 1; you have lost the old line, which is now passing through orchards to your left. However, after passing through the pretty hamlet of Selson and negotiated a very sharp bend, you arrive at the former and very obvious crossing over the road by the old Eastry to Richborough Port line. Go past the crossing then bear left* into the next field and hard left again to climb the embankment and follow the Eastry to Richborough Port line; very shortly a path goes off to the left, this being the first (or last) part of the line to and from Wingham. You're then able to follow this very picturesque path through the trees until you reach a dead end at the orchards. Retrace your steps to rejoin the road at the spot asterisked above and follow it to a T-junction; turn right here then shortly left along Gore Road to reach the pretty village of Eastry with an excellent range of amenities including a good bus service. As an alternative, of course, having hit the Richborough Port line you could continue along its course to Sandwich from the point asterisked above, following the instructions given in description 1 - the field you turn left into from the point asterisked above is marked with a ++ in description 1 for ease of reference.

Another walkable section of the old East Kent colliery line between Ash and Eastry; again Ash church can be seen in the background.

Some obstructions on the course of disused railways leave no scope for negotiation.
Left: near Headcorn (walk 10).
Below: near Paddock Wood (walk 9).

WALK 17 - **RAMSGATE - MARGATE**

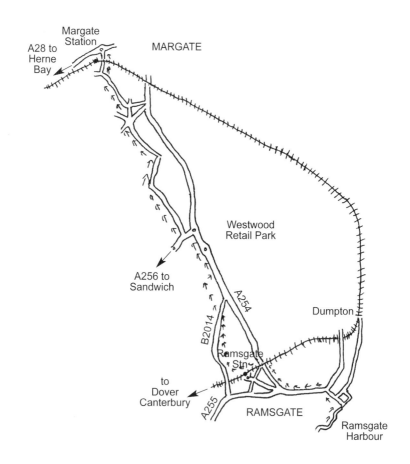

Scale: 2·6cm - 1km

WALK 17 - **RAMSGATE - MARGATE**

Length:	5.5 miles.
Start:	Ramsgate (harbour or station).
Finish:	Margate station.
Public Transport:	Regular trains serving Ramsgate and Margate from London Victoria via Faversham and from Canterbury via Sturry and Minster.
Refreshments:	Ramsgate (P,C,S); Westwood retail park (P,C,S); Margate (P,C,S).
Conditions:	This is sadly one of the least rewarding pieces of disused railway exploration in Kent. There is very little of the old lines to see, and the surroundings are generally uninteresting. It is one for the connoisseur only! If you do decide to give it a go, you won't need more than half a day to do it.

History

April 1846 saw the South Eastern Railway open a line from Canterbury to Ramsgate via Sturry and Minster, a line which still exists today, albeit the original terminus at Ramsgate (known as Ramsgate Town) was a little to the south-east of where Ramsgate station is sited today. This was the first railway incursion into the Thanet area of Kent. In December 1846 a line was then opened heading northwards from Ramsgate to Margate, and it is this that forms the principal subject matter of this chapter. A spur was subsequently built in order to facilitate through trains from Canterbury to Margate. Trains ran to a terminus in Margate that was very close to the seafront (just to the north-east of where Margate station stands today), and this terminus was subsequently to become known as Margate Sands.

The next significant development was in 1863 when the South Eastern Railway(SER)'s great rival, the London Chatham & Dover Railway(LCDR), completed a line which ran from west to east along the north Kent coast via Herne Bay to Margate. This included a new station for Margate which was firstly known as "Margate C & D" and subsequently Margate West, and which stood on the site of the present Margate station. The new LCDR line then continued over the SER line just south of Margate Sands and proceeded south-eastwards via another Margate station (East Margate, later becoming known as Margate East, and now defunct), Broadstairs and Dumpton Park, then embarking on a 1 in 75 cutting and entering a tunnel nearly a mile long to drop down to a station at Ramsgate by the waterfront, known as Ramsgate Harbour. This would certainly have been a great deal more convenient for passengers heading for the beach at Ramsgate than the SER station which was a good mile from the sea. The line opened on 5th October 1863. The next year, a spur was built by the LCDR at Margate just east of the SER line to accommodate an extra station for the town, but this was never used, being let to a catering firm who named it "Hall by the Sea."

Fast forward 60 years. By the 1920's, the line between Ramsgate Town and Margate Sands was enjoying a frequent service, with over 15 return journeys between the two towns on weekdays in 1922, and an even higher number of journeys between Margate West and Ramsgate Harbour via the tunnel. Timings were curious: if you missed the 8.38am from Broadstairs to Ramsgate Harbour you only had to wait 11 minutes for the next, but if you missed that, you would have to wait until 10.23 for the following train, with another one coming along less than 25 minutes later. However, major changes were in store. In July 1926, the LCDR line from Dumpton Park towards Ramsgate was realigned and continued to a point just north of the original Ramsgate Town station. A new station was opened at Ramsgate, and at the same time both the SER line from Ramsgate Town to Margate Sands and the tunnel route from Dumpton Park to Ramsgate Harbour were shut. The tunnel route reopened in 1936 as a pleasure railway and then became used as an air raid shelter during World War 2, reopening once more as a pleasure railway in 1946 and closing for good in 1965. The harbour terminus was turned into an amusement park but this was badly damaged by fire some years ago and the tunnel itself has now been sealed off. The "Hall by the Sea" spur at Margate was obliterated by the Dreamland fun park, itself now defunct, and the old line from Ramsgate Town to Margate is hardly followable at all, swallowed up by new development including an enormous retail park.

Walking the Lines

If you wish to inspect the route taken by the old line from Broadstairs and Dumpton to Ramsgate Harbour, make your way to the seafront at Ramsgate and follow Harbour Parade past East Pier to the land side of the Royal Victoria Pavilion. Here you can see the extensive cliffs under which the line was tunnelled; it emerged from the underground close to the lift which conveys pedestrians from the harbour area to the clifftop by Wellington Crescent. There really is no purpose in walking to the point where the old line emerged to join what is now the realigned route from Broadstairs to Ramsgate, as it is (was!) all underground. So get up to the clifftop, either by the lift or steps, walk along Wellington Crescent, effectively the clifftop road, then bear left onto the B2054 Victoria Road and forward along the A255 Boundary Road to the junction with the A254 Margate Road. Here turn right up the A254.

Now you have a choice. You could simply follow the A254 north-westwards, passing under the extant railway, and bear shortly left into Whitehall Road. Alternatively, you could turn left off the A254 immediately after joining it beyond the A255 junction and walk up Station Approach Road to follow the course the Canterbury-Ramsgate line originally took, in due course arriving at the present Ramsgate station. This will be the starting point if you don't wish to inspect the site of the Harbour station. Now, from immediately in front of the station entrance (with your back to the station itself), turn left and pass the advertising hoardings. Almost immediately turn left onto a signed concrete footpath which proceeds downhill, turns sharp left to pass under the extant railway, then bears very sharply right and heads north-eastwards to arrive at the A254 Ramsgate-Margate road. Turn left and follow it briefly to arrive at the left turning into Whitehall Road, and turn left to follow this road.

Proceed along Whitehall Road until you reach the second turning on the right, Hurst Grove. Looking left (south-eastwards) from here, you'll be

Warm September sunshine casts shadows of fencing that adjoins this path along the old Ramsgate-Margate line near the big Westwood retail park.

following with your eyes the course of the old line, while looking half-left, south-westwards, you'll be following with your eyes the course of the spur route from the (still extant) Canterbury-Ramsgate line. Both these old lines have been completely swamped by housing and also a large jumble of railway sidings and sheds servicing the existing line. You could turn right up Hurst Grove, the course of the old line immediately parallel with you to the left, but there are no traces of it now and there's no way forward;

accordingly, whether you've detoured up Hurst Grove or not, continue along Whitehall Road and turn right up St James' Avenue. It is hardly inspiring walking! Keep along St James' Avenue until it bends quite sharply left, and just beyond house number 105 turn right onto an alleyway that leads to a more open grassy area. On reaching it, bear left to walk towards Allenby Road. You are now briefly on the course of the old line; looking back, you can see the course it would have taken, but it has become inaccessible by virtue of the housing. Go on to Allenby Road, noting the course of the old line over the road through the back yards of the North Court housing development to the left (there's no bar to access but you can't get out the other end!), and turn left to reach a crossroads junction with Newington Road.

Turn right to follow Newington Road briefly, pass the infants' school, then immediately beyond the school turn left onto a clear path which follows the course of the old line. It's a pleasant popular path so you may not be on your own. It widens and becomes rougher before veering right and petering out at Highfield Road; turn left into Highfield Road then left again at the T-junction with Margate Road which you follow, passing extensive superstores to the left which have completely covered the course of the old line. You cross a roundabout and go forward to the next at Westwood Retail Park, a massive complex which is almost a town in itself. Turn left here, crossing the course of the old line, then first right into Nash Road, keeping the (inaccessible) course of the old line to your right and following Nash Road for just over a mile; although it's classed as a minor road it can be extremely busy and there's no pavement. As you begin to descend, now within sight of Margate, you'll notice a road on the right with barriers and a No Entry sign beside it. This is in fact an overbridge crossing of the old line, and by walking downhill a little past this road you should be able to scramble onto the line and follow it first back towards the retail park and then forward towards Margate. It's lovely walking but sadly there are only "dead ends:" impenetrable vegetation at the south end, and, at the north end, a bridge crossing that's no longer there. You're therefore forced back to Nash Road, following it on to a multi-road junction which you cross, bearing half-right into Tivoli Road and first left into Tivoli Park Avenue.

Now walk along Tivoli Park Avenue towards Margate. You have the course of the old line on the bank to your right; the bank is accessible initially but soon becomes impossible to negotiate further, so it's back to Tivoli Park Avenue which you follow, getting glimpses of the course of the old line between the houses to the right. You could bear right into Mere Gate, because by following it to its far east end and walking into the garage area beyond, you can glimpse the course of the "Hall by the Sea" spur route - however it is not followable at all, so you're forced back. Return to Tivoli Park Avenue and continue to the junction with All Saints Avenue. Turn hard right here and walk down towards the overbridge bearing the existing Margate-Broadstairs-Ramsgate railway; just before it you can detour right up a lane leading to an industrial estate, and you soon reach a jumble of vegetation to your right which marks approximately the course of the old line. Again, however, you're forced to return to the road. Now pass under the existing line and very soon reach a right-hand turn into a rather rundown multi-storey car park. By walking up the ramp straight ahead (beware - signs warn pedestrians not to walk along it) you will not only cross the course of the old line for the final time, but from the level concrete area at the top of the ramp you can look out across the rather pathetic remains of the Dreamland amusement park which shut in 2003 - the "Hall by the Sea" spur ran across the park which is now strictly out of bounds. Return to the road and follow it to a roundabout junction with the A28. By turning right here you'll soon pass a very conspicuous grey tower block, marking the site of Margate Sands station at the end of the old line, and a little beyond that you'll reach the very appropriately named Hall By The Sea Road which leads to the former entrance to the amusement park. This marked the end of the spur route. There is a real sense of neglect and dereliction about the surroundings, and it's possible that this whole area may be redeveloped in future - one hopes for the sake of the local economy that it will be. To reach Margate station, walk back to the A28 roundabout junction and turn half-left to walk up the station approach road; there's a café and restaurant immediately adjoining the station, as well as a station buffet, if you require refreshment before catching your train home.

Towards the end of the old line between Ramsgate and Margate, just off Nash Road.

AFTERWORD - OTHER DISUSED KENT RAILWAYS

As stated at the start of this book, there are a number of sections of disused railway in Kent that have not been included. These include the host of military, industrial, dockland and other non-passenger railways that were excluded from the Gazetteer in the South East England edition of H.P. White's Forgotten Railways series, and disused sidings, spurs and realignments of still existing parts of the passenger network. However this doesn't mean that some of these pieces of old line do not repay exploration, if only to see how much (or perhaps more to the point, how little) evidence of the former railway actually remains. Some of that exploration may be able to be undertaken on foot. One example is the old line linking the old Tovil station on the Paddock Wood-Maidstone West line with Tovil Goods which opened in 1886 and shut in 1977; part of the old railway bridge over the Medway can be seen, as well as a portion of embankment. However, some "exploration" may have to be limited to watching from the window of a train on an existing line. Sadly, as with much of the exploration of disused railways detailed in the main body of the text, you are likely to have just as much difficulty, if not a good deal more so, in accessing the old lines themselves, and in the context of industrial railways, your safety may be in danger if you explore old industrial sites without

As explained in the text, there are many sections of disused railway in Kent which fall outside the scope of this book. Here is the remnant of a bridge which carried a freight-only line that branched off the Paddock Wood-Maidstone West line at Tovil. This branch opened in 1886 and served local industries including a paper mill. Traces of the branch can still be seen today.

proper permission or precautions. Such exploration is anyway likely to be of greater interest to the railway historian than the railway walker. Maps showing all railways in Kent, past and present, are included in the Kent and Sussex edition of the Ian Allan Railways Of Britain series by Colin and David McCarthy, published in 2007, ISBN 9780711032224.

Although some spurs off existing lines, including those at Folkestone and Dover, have been shut in the comparatively recent past, it is 25 years since the last closure of a railway line in Kent on the passenger network (Grove Junction-Eridge). With the growth in popularity of rail travel and environmental pressures to use more sustainable forms of transport, it is to be hoped that there will be no more additions to the family of disused passenger lines in Kent in the future. Perhaps a more positive thing to hope for is that the local authorities and landowners can work together to open up a great deal more of the huge mileage of disused line in Kent for leisure use. A good start has been made with sections of the Canterbury-Whitstable and Tenterden-Headcorn lines now converted into footpaths, but so much more could still be done.

S.B. Publications publish a wide range of local interest books on Sussex.
For a free catalogue please write to:
S.B. Publications, 14 Bishopstone Road, Seaford, East Sussex BN25 2UB
or access our website on
www.sbpublications.co.uk